Radical Marriage:
Your Relationship as Your Greatest Adventure

by David and Darlene Steele

Radical Marriage: Your Relationship as Your Greatest Adventure

First Edition

Printed in the United States of America.

Published by RCN Press
a division of Relationship Coaching Institute
P.O. Box 111783, Campbell, CA 95011
888-268-4074
www.RelationshipCoachingInstitute.com
www.RCNpress.com

Library of Congress Cataloging-in-Publication Data

Steele, David A. (1957-), and Steele, Darlene, K. (1961-)
    Radical Marriage: Your Relationship as Your Greatest Adventure / 1st ed.

E-book ISBN: 978-0-9904612-1-0
Paperback ISBN: 978-0-9904612-2-7

Library of Congress Control Number: 2014949595

1. Marriage.   2. Relationships.   3. Communication.   4. Intimacy   I. Title

Genre: Non-fiction / Family & Relationships / Marriage

Attention Universities, Colleges, Churches, Professional Associations and other organizations: Quantity discounts are available on bulk purchases of this book. For more information please contact: support@relationshipcoachinginstitute.com

Relationship Experts Praise
Radical Marriage

"Radical Marriage provides clear ideas, easy strategies to follow, and a 'radical' new paradigm for creating the relationship of your dreams."
— Harville Hendrix, Ph.D. and Helen LaKelly Hunt, Ph.D. Co-authors of Making Marriage Simple

"Radical Marriage is for couples in good marriages who envision something wonderful for their future together. The Steeles have given us a manifesto and road map for marriage as a more perfect union."
— William J. Doherty, Ph.D., Professor of Family Social Science, University of Minnesota, author of Take Back Your Marriage: Sticking Together in a World That Pulls Us Apart

"Radical Marriage is an accessible and clear description of the steps for relationship success with many easy-to-follow strategies for making life and love better."
— Don Ferguson, Ph.D. author of Reptiles in Love and The Couples' Manual

"Is your marriage where you want it to be? This book will challenge you to take it to the next level, beyond where you ever thought it could be. Your marriage can be more – wonderfully more, extraordinarily more, radically more!"
— Greg and Priscilla Hunt, BetterMarriages.org

Table of Contents

About This Book

Before we get started, here are a few things we'd like you to know about this book:

- Much more than a self-help book, Radical Marriage is a movement to promote the evolution of committed relationships and save one of our most important social institutions from (perceived) obsolescence.

- Written by a couple, the term "we" is used in this book to refer to the authors and is not intended to include the members and staff of Relationship Coaching Institute.

- While gender specific terms are used for convenience such as "husband," "wife," "him" and "her," it is our full intention to be inclusive of all committed relationships of all gender and sexual orientations.

- We define "marriage" to be a formally committed lifetime relationship, whether legally recognized or not.

- The word "radical" in Radical Marriage refers to a dramatically new paradigm and does not mean a "do-anything-you-want-without-consequences" approach to marriage, as you'll soon discover in Radical Commitment (Chapter Two).

- Throughout this book are "Radical Actions" to help you start implementing the suggested strategies. These are intended to provide an idea of how to begin and are not a comprehensive list of everything you could do. If you need more support, ideas and guidance to implement the strategies in this book we suggest contacting a Radical Marriage Coach, Radical Marriage Mentor Couple, joining our Radical Marriage Online Community, or joining a

Radical Marriage Circle (see appendix).

- While Radical Marriage is a specific paradigm with distinct assumptions and suggested practices, it is our intention for you to take what fits and discard what doesn't. Many of the ideas in this book are challenging to most couples and what matters is that you co-create the Radical Marriage that fits best for you so that you can honestly and enthusiastically declare *We have a Radical Marriage!*

Introduction:
Beyond Happily Ever After

"What you conceive and believe, you can achieve"
—Napoleon Hill (paraphrased)

Napoleon Hill's "conceive, believe, achieve" quote is a powerful statement and a powerful truth. It says that we can go far beyond our self-imposed limits. But there's a flip side to those words—this also means that what you don't conceive or believe, you can't achieve.

As relationship coaches, our job is to help singles and couples who want to live happily ever after. It's a worthy goal and a worthy dream. But there are big limits to that dream:

1. You might have a *desire* (love) but not a clear idea, vision, or dream for what it looks like, <u>so you're stuck with what *is*</u>.

2. You might have a clear dream, but not really believe it's possible or realistic, <u>so you're stuck with what you'll allow yourself to have</u>.

3. You might believe it's possible, but your dream is limited to what you can actually envision, <u>so you're stuck with a narrow range of possibilities</u>.

This is where Radical Marriage comes in.

A New Paradigm for Marriage is Needed

As coaches, we're here to help you dream big, reach deep down, and uncover desires you didn't even know you had. Our role is to help you recognize and reach the next level of your dreams. This is especially important when it comes to relationships.

Most couples don't want an ordinary,
boring, routine relationship.

Most couples don't want an ordinary, boring, routine relationship. They want excitement, fun, closeness, love.

When we get married we make vows to be together until death do us part. That's a long time, and sadly, half of marriages don't or can't keep that commitment.

We have a dream or vision of how we want our life together to be, and we become unhappy if we're too far off track from that dream. If we don't believe our dream is possible we feel hopeless, stuck, and eventually leave the marriage, mentally, emotionally, and physically.

The current marriage rate stands at 51 percent, an all-time low, and according to recent surveys about 44 percent of adults under 30 believe that marriage is obsolete. And who can blame them? Looking around at their parents and others, they see more downsides than benefits. Thankfully, as they mature their attitude towards marriage gets warmer.

While it may be on the decline, marriage has many benefits and plays an important role in our society in the most inclusive way possible. What matters most is not your chosen lifestyle, but your life, with whomever you choose to live it. Marriage, in this context, refers to the level of commitment. There is a certain day, time, and place you can point to that says, "There, that's the moment we became committed for life."

We need a new paradigm of marriage as
a clear path to happiness and fulfillment.

No matter the terms or how you choose to define them, it's clear that it's time for the scope of marriage to evolve. We need a new paradigm of marriage as a clear path to happiness and fulfillment, rather than shackles holding us back from living life to the fullest.

The Radical Marriage Movement

---

rad•i•cal (adjective):
very different from the usual or traditional

Radical Marriage is not just a book or set of ideas and strategies; it's a movement. It's a way of doing and being. It's a cause, and it comes with great meaning behind it.

As we write this, fewer people are getting married; the divorce rate is at an all-time high, and a significant percentage of men and women view marriage as a quaint, obsolete anachronism. They equate it with being locked up in a cage. They view it as dull and routine, suffocating and destined for failure. One of the most popular internet matchmaking websites targets bored married people with over 21 million subscribers, specializing in infidelity with the slogan "Life is short. Have an affair". If marriage is to survive in our culture, this has to change. It's either evolve or die.

The good news is that there continues to be a strong desire for marriage. We recognize its inherent value and we are hard-wired for committed relationships. At the same time, we face an uphill battle due to conditioning and perception. Many people believe getting married means sacrifice and giving up some of the good things in life. And if they do get married and become bored and dissatisfied after a few years, they believe it's the institution of marriage itself that's holding them back.

The Paradox of Marriage

Our current challenges speak to an interesting paradox of marriage today. On the one hand, people view marriage as wholesome and desirable. On the other, they see it as old fashioned. People are attracted to marriage, but they are also afraid of it. People want the companionship and partnership of marriage, but they also believe it will take away their freedom and ultimately end in divorce. People seek the security of marriage, but they think it means they can no longer have a fun and exciting life.

We're here to open your eyes, rock your world, and change your reality about marriage.

Radical Marriage has been created to resolve this paradox and promote a much-needed paradigm shift. We're here to open your eyes, rock your world, and change your reality about marriage. Our intention is to introduce you to a new way of looking at marriage where you can never go back.

Marriage is an ancient institution rich with traditions and customs. As appealing as that may be, in today's modern culture, we want to forge our own path and live our life our way. We want to pursue our own destiny and go where our energy wants to go. We don't want to conform to how society wants us to be and we don't want to follow some predetermined path that our parents expect of us.

Our relationship can be the greatest adventure of our life. It can be the vehicle for experiencing the excitement and fulfillment that we have always wanted. We can only get so far on our own. To get the rest of the way, we need a committed partner.

A Radical Marriage is the platform we need to stand on firmly to deepen and evolve our relationship and experience life to the fullest. It's important because we need that security. We need a boat that doesn't leak. We need a car with a good engine and good tires. We need a solid foundation upon which we can build and grow.

Radical Marriage is a model of how we can leverage that foundation and security to have our relationship be our greatest adventure and achieve the kind of fulfillment and live the kind of life together that we couldn't possibly realize on our own. This is an attractive proposition, for sure, but it's not easy. What's easy is to do what everybody else does, or what has always been done in the past. A *Radical Marriage,* by contrast, takes effort, creativity and intention.

The good news is you don't have to do it alone. When you are part of a team, this journey becomes fun and exciting. Yes, it is something that you have to put some time and energy into, but then again, it is probably one of the best things that you *could* put your time and energy into. Every moment that you invest in your relationship and your marriage—and we use the word *invest* consciously—will pay off in a big way.

Evolution is Messy and Inevitable

Despite the rewards ahead, it is important to note that evolution is not clean and linear. It's messy. When we advance our values, abilities, and expectations too fast, we get out of control. Then we have to back up a bit, start over, and learn how to integrate the changes into our life. This is true for technology, it's true for lottery winners and job promotions, and it's true for the culture at large (remember the 60's?). It's especially true for relationships and marriage.

12

Still, evolution is inevitable. We can resist change and hang on to things the way they were, but we are going to lose if we try. So, we might as well embrace evolution and help it along so that we can maximize and optimize the growth and opportunity. That's the purpose behind Radical Marriage.

Rather than equating a committed relationship with a loss of freedom, giving up who we are, who we want to be, and how we want to live, Radical Marriage is a form of empowerment. This new paradigm transforms marriage from the mentality of grudging sacrifice to the platform for life's greatest adventure. It brings us from a mindset of misery or boredom and the reality of high risk of divorce to a gateway to excitement and fulfillment far beyond where we could have gone on our own.

It is fundamental to the survival of one of our most important social institutions to be able to view marriage differently instead of practicing failure or throwing it away, and Radical Marriage serves that purpose. It's about evolving marriage to where it needs to go. After all, any social institution, marriage or otherwise, that seems dull, routine, and boring, with a high chance of failing, is not going to survive. And we as a culture will not survive without marriage, for all the reasons why marriage works.

As the secure basis of a family that raises children to be fully functional, well-adjusted adults, marriage is crucial. It creates the necessary safety and stability for a truly committed relationship and family. We are wired for it. We survive and thrive best in it (see Benefits of a Committed Relationship in the appendix).

13

You Don't Bring Me Flowers Anymore

Neil Diamond and Barbra Streisand sang a duet that is the lament of many married couples under the old paradigm:

You don't bring me flowers
You don't sing me love songs
You hardly talk to me anymore
When you come through the door
At the end of the day

I remember when
You couldn't wait to love me
Used to hate to leave me

Now after lovin' me late at night
When it's good for you
And you're feeling alright
Well, you just roll over
And you turn out the light

You don't bring me flowers anymore

This is the default for marriage if we don't do anything about it. At this point many people believe that if they can't change their marriage or their partner, the solution is to change partners. But if you have problems or if you find things getting stale and boring in your marriage, it doesn't mean that you throw it out or surf the internet for an affair. It just means that your marriage needs to evolve. Rather than leaving it or bypassing it to go forward alone, you and your partner can now embrace a new model of marriage together; one in which you maximize your chances of experiencing your greatest adventure, pursuing your dreams and living a life of fulfillment—becoming far more successful as a team than you could by yourself.

Use this book as a road map to discover your truth, explore the possibilities of your dream relationship, and implement the strategies described in these pages to live *beyond* happily ever after. As you read this book try to put aside any fears and resistance that may arise, open your mind and allow yourself to consider a radical approach to achieving happiness and fulfillment in your life, relationships, and marriage. After all, unless you've seen or experienced something, it can be difficult to envision. And unless you can conceive it, you can't achieve it.

Thank you, Napoleon Hill.

We're in this Together

As key players within Relationship Coaching Institute, this material is unusual for us. Not because the topic is foreign territory—it's not; it's just that typically when we address something, it comes from years of study and experience. It's about what *is*. This particular subject, however, is fresh. It's still under exploration and development. It's more about what *will be*.

What you are about to explore is raw and real. It is authentic and it is unique. It is a departure from the norm. It is, by definition, *Radical*. It is as much a discovery for us as it is for you—we are in this together. It is exciting and scary at the same time. It is, we believe, the secret to *living beyond happily ever after*.

The Dirty Little Secret of Relationship Happiness

All couples start out with the most basic of intentions. They start single and want to meet someone. They want to fall in love. They want to be happy. They want a *good* relationship. But is *good* really enough? Perhaps it was in the past, where a *good* relationship was commonly defined as not having problems. In today's world, however, couples seek fulfillment in their relationship, not the simple absence of problems.

In today's world, good just isn't good enough.

No, in today's world, *good* just isn't good enough.

That's not to say that *good* can't be fulfilling—for a while. Even *good* relationships are exciting when new. But happiness is a moving target, and *good* relationships can quickly become dull and routine. Little problems of everyday living pile up and interfere with the closeness and intimacy that we really want.

As things get stale in our relationship we tell ourselves: *This is as close as I can get to living happily ever after*, while deep down we're asking, *Is this all there is?* We feel selfish, ungrateful, unfaithful and unrealistic for wanting more for our life and relationship. We stick with *good*. *Good* works. *Good* gets us by.

Here's the dirty little secret of relationship happiness: *Good* can become suffocating. *Good* can turn to agony. *Good* can lead to heartache if the relationship is stuck in routine and not continuing to evolve. *Good* can erode your quality of life. *Good* does not equal fulfillment.

Dreaming is for sleeping, but your dreams are for living life to the fullest. This means pushing the envelope with a partner. You are much more capable of reaching your potential in a couple relationship if you realize a fulfilling relationship is a journey, not a destination. The problem is that most of us can't see beyond the norm of what other couples do, so the journey stalls. The good news is that there's an answer.

Raising the Bar for Couple Relationships

As of this moment, right now as you're reading this, the bar officially has been raised. We have known for some time that having a great couple relationship is one of life's greatest adventures. What's different is that we are beginning to understand that to fully realize a relationship's potential, we need to look _beyond_ happily ever after; we need to get *radical*.

This is new territory in the field of relationships.

This is new territory in the field of relationships. And since each relationship is unique, your *radical relationship* will be unique to you and your partner. You and your partner must be pioneers in your life and relationship and discover your uncharted territory together. Sure, we relationship coaches can provide you with

17

support, skills, and strategies to guide you, but the journey is yours to take.

Here are five key ideas to keep in mind as you get started:

1. Your *dream* is what you can currently conceive, but you can go far beyond that.

2. To go beyond, you must be aware that *you don't know what you don't know*. You must be open to possibilities and be willing to continually progress forward into new territory with your partner.

3. "Radical" is not for everyone. Doing so requires a good, strong partnership and a willingness to embrace the journey, the learning, and the adventure. Instead of seeking comfort, tradition, and familiarity, you must be willing to be a pioneer. But if your partner drags their feet, be patient and don't try to do it alone—a big part of the adventure is doing it together, especially when it's challenging.

When you get to where you're striving,
you can see more, do more, and want more.

---

4. The dream *beyond happily ever after* further reveals itself as you progress. Each step forward allows you to see more possibilities. In that sense, there is no such thing as *achieving* a dream. When you get to where you're striving, you can see more, do more, and want more. You continue striving.

5. A Radical Marriage requires a leap of faith and a willingness to enter and embrace the unknown. There's a great scene from *Indiana Jones and the Last Crusade* that illustrates this: Indy reaches a huge chasm that he must cross and he isn't sure what to do. It's only after he takes that first, frightening step into the abyss that he discovers the path across. Like the scene in the movie, embracing your fears and not letting them hold you back is

a big theme in this book.

As Eleanor Roosevelt once said--
Do one thing every day that scares you.

Or, as Buzz Lightyear put it so succinctly-
To infinity and beyond!

Chapter One:
Is Radical Marriage Right For You?

David's Story

The concept of *beyond happily ever after* has consumed my thoughts for some time. When I was a kid my parents divorced. They were very unhappy people, both individually and with each other, which made my home life very unhappy. My escape was getting out of the house.

As I explored my community and went to school, observing other couple and family relationships showed me the possibilities in life. They showed me how great and how miserable things can be. I really *got* that relationships are keys—keys to joy or misery.

Human beings are social creatures and relationships come quite naturally to us. You would think that we would be able to make them work. It's not so easy. While the uncertainty of relationships makes life juicy, it does little to inherently improve the dynamic between the people you interact with on a daily basis.

There are seven billion people on this planet. Some of them are easy for you to get along with and some of them you would love to have as your friend. Others are just plain difficult for you to be around. On top of it all you have family relationships to deal with, which forms the basis of a whole new set of challenges.

And then there's marriage.

Learning from Experience

Most of us don't want to go through life alone.

Most of us don't want to go through life alone. We want to live happily ever after with the love of our life. We want that one special person or soul mate, or whatever term speaks to you, to share the human experience with. It's a particular journey which has always fascinated me because of my unhappy family and childhood that fueled my interest in becoming a marriage and family therapist. So I did.

I went to school, completed my internships, passed my exams, got my license, and for many years I was in private practice as a couples therapist. Most of the couples that came to me were on the verge of divorce. They were unhappy together, typically had one foot out the door, and were trying therapy as a last resort. For my part, I tried to save their marriage. Despite my best efforts, it only worked about half the time. They got divorced anyway. So I sought more training. My 50% success rate had me questioning my own abilities and skills. *Well, shoot, if I'm not able to save their marriages, I can't be a very good therapist.*

Looking around at what my colleagues were doing, I discovered that they weren't having any better success. While this made me feel better about myself and my abilities, it did little to quell my passion for helping people. It wasn't okay with me that so many relationships were failing—and so many *marriages.*

As a kid who grew up in a divorced home, a life-long bond was something to which I aspired. So when I got married, as young as I was at the time, I intended to honor those vows. I wanted to be together for life. I wanted to live happily ever after. It didn't work out that way. My first marriage lasted ten years and ended in divorce.

There I was, a brand new marriage and family therapist, going through a divorce. It was not an easy time in my life or my profession. In fact it was devastating. But I was determined not to give up. I gave it a second try and got married again. That one, too, lasted around ten years and ended in divorce.

I am the worst, most inadequate failure
at this relationship thing in the world.

I am the worst, most inadequate failure at this relationship thing in the world, I thought. I even began to have thoughts of giving up on my dream. Not only that, I began to have thoughts of giving up on *myself*. I began to resign myself to being alone forever. *I'm jinxed or cursed somehow*, I thought. *As much as I want this for myself it's not going to happen. As much as I want this for other people, it's just not working*.

Doubling Down

Not only did I not give up, I doubled down on my commitment and dedicated my life to studying relationships and helping other people. Regardless of how my own life was working out, I wanted to help others live happily ever after.

In the 90's I was blessed to discover the emerging field of coaching. As a result, I ended up founding Relationship Coaching Institute. I saw coaching as the future for relationships. As a therapist I recognized that trying to fix something that's already broken is not necessarily the best strategy. Addressing something before it breaks, however, can yield tremendous results. That's coaching, and I reveled in its possibilities.

For me, entering the coaching profession and applying my passion and training to coaching relationships was a no-brainer. More than that, it was my salvation. I went all in. I looked around for training programs or mentors, anything or anybody who could teach me how to apply this new-found methodology to relationships. There was nothing. So I took it upon myself to figure it out. I learned how to do it, and then started teaching others. That was the birth of Relationship Coaching Institute and led me to where I am today.

I couldn't take my clients beyond "good"
since I couldn't see beyond good.

As a therapist, I devoted my profession to helping people achieve a good relationship. Even when I succeeded, that was as far as it went. I couldn't take my clients beyond "good" since *I* couldn't *see* beyond good. Once my clients were no longer in danger of getting divorced, they stopped coming and I felt good about my work. I thought my work was done, because I didn't know any better. I was never trained in what to do after you help a couple have a "good" relationship.

My eyes were opened reading Gay and Katie Hendricks' book, *Conscious Loving*. It inspired me with possibilities. It helped me see that there is a spiritual level to relationships, a level beyond what we can see and know. I became aware that the couple relationship is the ultimate adventure in personal growth and in living life to the fullest.

Of course, it's not simply a matter of partnership itself. You can partner with somebody and your life can be exciting and fulfilling, or you can partner with somebody and your life can be miserable. As a relationship coach, I help people not just find the love of their life, but have a fulfilling and exciting life. That's what *Radical Marriage* is all about, and much of it rides on the notion that *what you see, depends on where you're standing and where you're looking.*

What You See Depends Upon Where You're Standing and Where You're Looking

For a long time, the reality in my marriage and family therapy office was struggling couples. So the best I could see was getting them to *good.* That's also what I wanted for myself. Again, about half the couples crumbled, and I got divorced *twice* during that period.

Fast forward to Relationship Coaching Institute, exploring relationship coaching and new possibilities for relationships, and I'm standing in a different place and looking in a different direction. I applied to my own life what I learned about relationships and about singles, and I developed a whole relationship coaching program. I wrote a book for singles called *Conscious Dating,* exploring a few fundamental questions: How do you find the love of your life when you're single? How can you set yourself up for success? How can you live *happily ever after* from a standing start when you're single?

I applied these questions and philosophies to myself and found the love of my life, my soul mate, Darlene. We've been married now for seven years. She is a registered nurse, and she ended up leaving her profession to work with me at Relationship Coaching Institute. She is our Chief Operating Officer and runs everything behind the scenes at RCI. She is coauthor of this book and a tremendous value to our members. Together, we are having the grandest time exploring the possibilities for relationships.

Darlene and I also launched a web TV program called Let's Get Real (www.gettingreal.tv), where we address people's relationship problems and challenges and explore the look and feel of radical relationships. We have been exploring these concepts for ourselves and wanted to share them with our viewers in an open format. We developed Radical Marriage through our relationship as we went along and I could not have done it by myself. I also could not have done this as a marriage and family therapist. I'm doing this now as a relationship coach and as somebody who finally has the relationship and lifestyle that I dreamed about and desired.

*What you see depends upon where you're standing
and where you're looking.*

So whether you're standing in a place where you feel *happy* and satisfied with a clear view of an even brighter future, or you're in a place where you feel frustrated and unfulfilled with only darkness on the horizon, that's your reality. What you see depends upon where you're standing and where you're looking.

You Have a Choice

The beauty of it all—and I couldn't see this before—is that we have a choice where we stand and where we look. We can stand in the belief that we will never live happily ever after or that our partner is who they are and they won't change and therefore we are stuck. Or we can stand in the possibility that a Radical Marriage is absolutely possible and we are going to do everything we can to make it happen. We can look at possibilities rather than limits. What you see depends upon where you're standing and where you're looking. It's a powerful concept, and you absolutely have a choice about that.

In exercising that choice, for the purposes of this book, we're not going to address dysfunctional relationships and what to do when one partner is not on board and doesn't want to do something. If this is your situation, you're not ready for Radical Marriage.

There are many qualified, talented marriage and family therapists, social workers, and counselors who specialize in helping couples in trouble. Here we're not addressing how to fix a problematic relationship; we're focusing on the possibilities for a highly exceptional relationship.

Darlene's Story

When David suggested we write a book together about Radical Marriage, my first reaction was *I'm not a relationship expert, who am I to co-author a book about marriage?* But as we explored the concept further and started working on this project, my contribution became clear. In a way, it's better that I don't have a professional background in relationships because it frees me to look at things differently, from the end user's point of view, and not be constrained by academic study or clinical training.

It's not like I'm a blank slate when it comes to relationships.

Living in Possibility

All of my life I've been fascinated by how the world works and am naturally curious, especially about psychology. From the time I was a teenager and questioned "Why is everyone so stupid?!" I have been fascinated with what it means to be human. I took every psychology course offered in high school and Psychology 101 was the first college course I signed up for. I read everything I could get my hands on.

---

*What we learn from books, teachers or experts
is often the current wisdom of the day.
But, what else is there?*

But my curiosity has always been deeper than simply to learn *what is.* I've always been aware of the potential of *what could be.* What we learn from books, teachers or experts is often the current wisdom of the day. But, what else is there?

If "x" and "y" are true, couldn't we do "z" instead?
What else is there?
What if we…?
What would happen if I…?

26

To me, this is what makes life exciting. I love the idea of discovering what's around the bend that you can't yet see.

Letting Go of Fear

Fear seems to hold people back—especially when it's about themselves. Great strength comes from truly accepting ourselves for who we are, but it's hard to acknowledge and accept our perceived flaws and weaknesses.

I became, and still am, emotionally fearless.

A pivotal moment for me was during my Psych rotation in nursing school. Each morning before rounds the class would meet in a conference room and our instructor had us share what we were learning, thinking or feeling. We were encouraged to be open about ourselves as was expected of our psychiatric patients. I embraced this exercise and had never been so open before in my life—just laying out all of my fears of inadequacy and more. And I realized it was okay. What at first felt scary turned out not to be so scary at all. In fact, it was freeing and the possibilities that opened up were intoxicating. I saw how my fears were holding me back, and in that moment I completely let go and can honestly say that I became, and still am, emotionally fearless.

I Married My Father

My relationship story started out quite differently than David's. My parents had what appeared to be a pretty typical marriage for the times. My Mom was a housewife and my Dad the breadwinner. My father loved us, there was no doubt about that. But, we certainly didn't have the fairytale. Our family was extremely father-centric and revolved around his moods and what he wanted. We all typically went along with it, but if we didn't, he would raise his voice to keep us in line, including my Mom. The whole family catered to his desires to keep him calm and happy.

I spent a lot of time and energy trying to get my mom to stand up for herself. It made me angry that my sweet mother's needs were put on the back burner. So I would often ask her "Why do you put up with it?!"

Ironically, I ended up marrying a man with similar traits as my father. I met my first husband at work. We had a similar sense of humor and spent a lot of time laughing and having fun together. By this time I had dated a number of young men and had a couple of year-long relationships. One thing they had in common was they were all nice guys and I never argued with any of them. Ever. But, within a few weeks of meeting my husband, we argued, a lot. And I cried, a lot. And that pattern repeated itself over and over for two decades and raising a family of two children. Funny how, like my mother, I accepted the situation for the sake of the family and felt responsible to make him happy, trying to "be better" so we wouldn't argue.

I guess I wasn't successful—we divorced 23 years later.

From Fantasy to Reality

For me the concept of Radical Marriage began many years ago—long before I met David. During my first marriage I imagined what a great marriage would be. I imagined waking up each morning with a feeling of peace knowing that my partner and I would work together to create an incredible, fulfilling life.

I knew we would have mutual respect and a shared vision. I fantasized about being able to talk about anything and really listen to each other. I imagined being passionately in love.

I knew that type of marriage was possible—and I really wanted it.

I still remember the exact moment when I realized that my dream was unfolding in front of me. David and I had been dating a short time and were already starting to talk about a life together. I was driving over to his house one afternoon and the realization hit me with a wave of excitement and peace. *Oh, my gosh–this is it! This is the start of what I've always wanted.*

Fast forward about five years. By this time, David and I were not only married, but pretty much together 24/7 as I left my job as a nurse to work with him full-time.   There wasn't any doubt what a great marriage we had, and it was everything I had dreamed of.

Actually it was more than I had dreamed of.

Discovering my Superpower

We often hear people say *"It's complicated"* when explaining why they tolerate a bad relationship. Relationships are complex. They aren't linear and nothing happens in isolation.

I came to realize that *"It's complicated"* also accurately describes the possibilities in a good marriage. While I had been dreaming about this for two decades, I couldn't have anticipated how we would evolve as partners or exactly what path our life together would take us.

Yes, marriage is complicated, wonderfully complicated.

Just as a challenging relationship can hold you back from accomplishing wonderful things or reaching your potential, a strong relationship gives you the strength and platform to grow in ways that you couldn't on your own. Yes, marriage is complicated, wonderfully complicated.

So, I'm proud of my contributions to Radical Marriage. I recognize that I hold the space for exploring untapped potential and discovering and embracing possibilities. And I am clear that I was put on this earth to look deeply and fearlessly inside myself and my marriage, to explore what else is possible and do my part in paving the way for others.

I've been preparing for Radical Marriage all of my life.

This is what I'm great at, this is my superpower, and I've been preparing for Radical Marriage all of my life.

Jack and Jill's Story

In the typical love story, two people meet, fall in love, and live happily ever after. As we touched upon earlier, this could just as easily be Jack and Jack or Jill and Jill—your soul mate is your choice—but for the sake of example and at the risk of using a cliché, we're going with Jack and Jill.

Scene One: Jack and Jill Meet

Jack and Jill are single. They find each other, meet, and something clicks. There's an attraction. You have been hoping to find somebody and when you finally do and it seems like a relationship is a possibility, it is exciting. Your hormones, thoughts, and fantasies are going, and now you have the reality right in front of you and it's fantastic.

Every choice we make has consequences...

The choices we make in this moment determine what happens in the next moment, which ultimately determines your outcome. You would think this is somewhat intuitive. And to many, it is. Every choice we make has consequences, and we must be more conscious of our choices to make them effectively so we get what we want. The problem is, no matter how obvious that may be, we often have a difficult time doing it. (We, the authors, are raising our hands here.)

When we're attracted to someone, we often miss or overlook red flags. Despite the presence of serious problems, we tend to believe that love conquers all and that we can "make" it work. Similarly, many people brush problems aside because they genuinely see value in what they have and don't want to be alone.

The 80% Relationship

The phenomenon of overlooking issues puts people in what we call the 80% relationship, where 80% is great and 20% is a challenge. That 20%, however, is what often dooms the relationship. It's problematic, it's unsolvable, and you can't live with it over the long term.

A spinoff of the doomed 80% relationship is the salvageable 80% relationship, where the remaining 20% is composed of stuff that can be solved. It can be fixed. It's something you can live with over the long term. The choices we make here, when we first meet somebody and decide whether or not to see them again, are crucial.

Scene Two: Jack and Jill Fall in Love

This is where things get exciting. You have met somebody and you have made a connection. The hormones are going and the fantasies and desires are in overdrive. You are having experiences together that bring you closer together; maybe you are even having sex. You are falling in love.

Sometimes people interpret attachment as love.

Sometimes people interpret *attachment* as *love*. Well, you can be attached to your favorite pair of sweatpants, too, but that doesn't necessarily make it love. Still, we human beings are imperfect and we have this instinct and desire to partner. We feel what we feel and it feels overwhelming and strong and sometimes we interpret that as love and we want it to work.

Pre-commitment

The law of inertia compels us to stay together and try to make things work. We call this stage in a relationship the "pre-commitment" stage. It's a wonderful and exciting stage, and it's also an important stage to decide, *Yes or No? Is this the right relationship for me? Should I make a commitment here? Is this going to work for me? Is it going to meet all of my requirements? My needs and wants? Am I going to be able to have the relationship and life that I want with this person? Should I stay or go? Yes or no?*

People at this stage, when they're falling in love, don't want to break up and move on. However, it's worth noting that if the relationship doesn't appear to be a good fit, even though breaking up is hard to do, the decision to move on is much easier here than later. We have learned the hard way that the fit of a relationship is *everything*.

If you go to the store and you get a jacket that's too small or too big, it's always going to bug you. The jacket could keep you warm, but if it's not the right fit, it's never going to feel quite right. It's the same with the fit in a relationship. If it's not the right fit, it's never going to feel quite right.

Scene Three: Jack and Jill Get Married

This is where Jack and Jill decide to make a commitment. This, too, is exciting, because for many people it's the realization of a dream. There is security in knowing that you have your special person now, you are not alone anymore, and that you and your partner are going to be together for the rest of your life. You get married or have a commitment ceremony. You take vows and have lots of hopes and dreams together. Over time, when those hopes and dreams don't get realized and problems and frustrations build up, it can become not so exciting anymore.

Scene Four: Jack and Jill Become Routine

Jack and Jill, now a married couple, have been together for a while and everything has been exciting up to this point. Here, things are getting routine and comfortable. This is what we call a *good* relationship. Sure, at times the routine is frustrating or not so great, but it's their routine and they are comfortable with it. This is common for couples because they don't know any different. The road to eventual divorce starts at this stage for many couples when they recognize the presence of problems and are unable to solve them.

Scene Five: Jack and Jill Have a Good Marriage and Live Happily Ever After

Like many couples, Jack and Jill met and fell in love. They got married and they live happily ever after. They believe that if you don't have problems in your relationship, then you have a *good* relationship. They are comfortable. Their basic needs are met. They have shelter, air, food, and all their basic physical and emotional needs are satisfied.

If the relationship ever needs something, if it's been a while since they have been on a date, if they have some confusion over paying a bill or not, if there is some frustration or an argument, then they focus on their relationship as needed, in a reactive way. It's what most people do. In this state, compromise is often the primary strategy for making the relationship work.

If you are not moving forward, you are moving backward.

The problem is that if the only time you focus on your relationship is when it's needed, and if you are comfortable and being comfortable means that you don't put effort into things, eventually you become uncomfortable. It's as if you have a plant that you are not watering. After a while it wilts and dies. It's the same with your life and your relationship. When you are not nurturing your life and your relationship they tend to atrophy. Anything standing still is not going to stay the exact same way forever, because things always

33

change. If you are not moving forward, you are moving backward. If you are not growing, you are dying. There might not be any problems now, but if you don't put some effort into your relationship, you are going to have problems later.

Compromise (aka lose-lose)

In David's first marriage, before he knew any better, his primary strategy for making his marriage work was compromise. As an example, he and his wife always compromised on movies. She loved animal movies about horses, cats, dogs, dolphins; real and animated. She also wanted to watch love stories—chick flicks. But it was hard for him to sit through that stuff. He loved action-adventure movies and sci-fi, which she hated.

As a result of their different tastes in movies, they compromised. So for ten years of that marriage, David saw nothing but dramas and comedies. It wasn't until he divorced that he caught up on Star Wars, Star Trek, Indiana Jones, and other great movies. Essentially, he had given up a part of who he was for the sake of the relationship.

If you rely too much on compromise and are constantly meeting in the middle, giving up what you really want while your partner is doing the same thing, it's lose-lose. Neither of you are happy or fulfilled. Granted, if you do that every once in a while about something important, it's okay. If you do that all the time, on movies, restaurants, sex, you name it, you are not really living happily ever after; just ever after, unhappily.

Unfortunately, this is often the default. It's what most people do and what most people call a *good* marriage.

But there's another option.

Radical Marriage

As coaches, often we ask our clients, "Well, what do you want?" Underneath that is, "What would make you happy? What would make you feel good? What would make you truly satisfied with your life?"

---

*What would make you ecstatically,
radically happy beyond your wildest dreams?*

Now, we're asking a different question. We're going beyond *good*. We're going <u>beyond</u> happily ever after. We want to know what would make you ecstatically, radically happy beyond your wildest dreams.

Remember: What you see depends upon where you're standing and where you're looking. If all you see is *good*, and ask, *How can I have a good relationship? How can I have a good life?* Then that is as far as you are going to go. We don't just want good. We want *extraordinary*. We want a *radical* life, and along with that, a *Radical Marriage*.

Three Kinds of Dreams

There are three kinds of dreams. There are the ones that you are aware of, the ones that you are unaware of, and the ones that evolve.

Dreams that you are aware of are the ones that are on your conscious mind. These are the ones that you can see and that you know. It's like the tip of the iceberg poking through the water. Accomplishing these dreams gives you a *good* life.

Dreams that you are unaware of rest beneath the surface. They're there, but they're not readily visible. The cool thing is that once you start achieving your dreams, then you start uncovering more. It's an important concept to living beyond happily ever after. It is not until you get there that you can even see it and achieve it, which in turn helps you see and achieve even more. Once you have achieved *good* then you are ready for *radical*.

Our dreams evolve as we achieve them.

Dreams that evolve take more time to develop. As human beings, we change and evolve over time. What we wanted when we were twenty is different from what we want when we are thirty, forty, and fifty. Our dreams evolve as we achieve them, which is a good thing. It's not like we climb the mountain and reach the summit and then that's it. There's another mountain, and another mountain, and another mountain after that. To some people that may be a discouraging thought: *What? You mean that I'm never going to get there?* Others have a different take. To us, the fact that there are always other challenges and adventures ahead is what makes life exciting.

This doesn't mean that you have to live an extreme lifestyle and jump out of airplanes, but it does mean that if you focus on possibilities and allow yourself to go beyond good, happy, or okay, then life becomes exciting. Life becomes fresh, and you'll never become bored. You'll always be challenged and you'll always be alive.

The key to living beyond happily ever after is to recognize and accept that life is a journey, not a destination. It's not finding somebody, getting married and then, if you're lucky, you have a *good* relationship where you are content and comfortable. A Radical Marriage requires you to continually evolve with your dreams and with your partner.

What makes you happy today is not exactly what's going to make you happy tomorrow.

If you just stay comfortable you are going to go backward. You are going to end up being bored, at the very least. "Beyond happily ever after" means you embrace life as a journey that is ever evolving. What makes you happy today is not exactly what's going to make you happy tomorrow.

We need to take responsibility for our life, our relationship, and our fulfillment, and be willing to embrace that journey. Sure, it's challenging, but again, that is the spice of life. For us, this is where we live as relationship coaches, because it's what we want for ourselves and it's what we want to support you to do.

What's clear, and one of the things we've learned along the way, is that no one is successful alone. You cannot achieve the success and happiness and fulfillment in your life that you want all by yourself. It doesn't necessarily mean you need a coach, but it does mean you will need support or mentoring or a team on your side. Please don't do this alone. Please don't think you can do this alone. This is a big shift for the independent lone rangers that our culture promotes.

What Does a Radical Marriage Look Like?

With all of the possibilities swirling around, you may be trying to form that picture in your mind: *What does a Radical Marriage look like?* There really is no pre-set image. You and your partner get to define it for yourselves. That's the beauty of it. Still, you can see glimpses of it in other couple relationships. They're the ones that seem incredibly connected and in love, long after their honeymoon. They're the couples that inspire you to think, *I want to be like THAT!*

Have you ever had that experience? Do you know any couples like that?

When you step into the unknown and view your life and marriage as a constantly evolving adventure, when you're living on the edge just a little bit each day, you know you're getting closer. It takes work and ingenuity. Just like good physical health requires discipline to eat well and exercise regularly, a Radical Marriage requires continual effort, by both partners, in six fundamental areas, which are included in the chapters of this book:

1. Radical Commitment (Chapter 2):
Beyond your marriage vows, you both are absolutely 100% committed to your marriage, no matter what, and you are as committed to your partner's happiness as your own. You each take 100% responsibility for the relationship, your experience in the relationship and for your outcomes in the relationship.

2. Radical Communication (Chapters 3-6):
You know how to effectively exchange information so that it is thoroughly understood, and you know how to assert your needs, resolve differences and conflict to get on with the serious business of fulfilling your dreams together.

3. Radical Intimacy (Chapter 7):
You are completely transparent to your partner, you don't censor yourself or hold anything back. You share all your thoughts, feelings, wants, needs, fantasies and desires.

4. Radical Romance (Chapter 8):
You continually express your love, appreciation, attraction and adoration for your partner in words and actions and don't take your relationship for granted or allow passion to be replaced by routine.

5. Radical Sex (Chapter 9):
Beyond satisfying physical urges, you consciously seek and experience emotional, physical, and spiritual connection every day, continually exploring new ways to express love and pleasure your partner and allowing yourself to be loved and pleasured.

6. Radical Living (Chapter 10):
Beyond survival and comfort, you consciously design your lifestyle together, develop your shared vision and goals, devote time and resources to realizing your dreams in each moment together as well as prioritizing your goals and preparing for your future. You are aware of how short your time is on this planet and savor each precious moment of life and being together.

Characteristics of a Radical Marriage

*A Radical Marriage has partners who consider
their relationship their greatest, most important asset.*

Here are the primary characteristics of a Radical Marriage in our opinion:

1. A Radical Marriage is unique to each couple.
2. A Radical Marriage is absolutely committed.
3. A Radical Marriage is consciously co-created.
4. A Radical Marriage is driven by shared values and vision.
5. A Radical Marriage has intentional relationship rituals and practices.
6. A Radical Marriage is always evolving and challenging its partners.
7. A Radical Marriage has partners who always make decisions in connection with each other.
8. A Radical Marriage has partners who prioritize each other's needs and happiness.
9. A Radical Marriage has partners who take responsibility for their own needs and experience.
10. A Radical Marriage is inclusive and a role model and source of support for their family and community.
11. A Radical Marriage has partners who don't settle for "stuck," seeking creative solutions to their relationship challenges and get outside support as needed from friends, family, community, mentors, and professionals.
12. A Radical Marriage is 100% positive and "I can't", "I won't", "It's impossible", and "It's your fault" are not in its vocabulary.
13. A Radical Marriage relies on compromise as a last resort for resolving differences and is rarely needed.
14. A Radical Marriage has partners who consider their relationship their greatest, most important asset and source of fulfillment, meaning and adventure.

Is a Radical Marriage For You?

Radical Marriage isn't for everyone. It requires a strong relationship, so if yours is struggling, focusing on functional basics must be your priority. Radical Marriage requires a willingness to take risks, overcome resistance and experience a bit of fear, which can induce stress and anxiety when you're more wired for comfort and security. It requires inviting and embracing evolution and change, which is against the grain for those who crave routine.

Radical Marriage requires TWO willing participants, so if your partner isn't on the same page, that's where you must start. It requires growth, effort, and learning; while strongly desired by some, others would rather watch TV, drink beer, and fall asleep on the couch.

Radical Marriage is for couples with a good relationship who strongly believe that they are together for a reason, which is to experience life to the fullest through their relationship.

If you're still reading this, chances are good that a Radical Marriage is for you.

Now that you can conceive it, let's take a more detailed look at how to *create your ultimate relationship, live beyond happily ever after,* and achieve a *Radical Marriage.*

Chapter Two: Radical Commitment

Commitment is the glue that makes marriage work.

If there's one thing we've learned—and the research backs this up—it's that commitment is the glue that makes marriage work.

When you take vows and stick to them, you are on the right course. When you give yourself completely to your partner, you have found the right formula. When you are all-in, you find ways to stay together. When you are 100% committed, you accept and embrace your partner unconditionally. If a *Radical Marriage* is what you seek, any less than *Radical Commitment* just won't do.

If even one partner in the relationship has an 80% commitment, you are opening yourselves up for trouble. Even if you have a *good* relationship with less than 100% commitment your marriage will end up getting sabotaged. *Well, you know, I'm here as long as it's going to meet my needs. If it doesn't work out I can always leave.* Mental and emotional exit strategies tend to become self-fulfilling.

Radical Commitment requires 100% investment, physically and emotionally, in attitude and behavior. It's a state where you're not even looking at other partners, you're not even thinking about other partners, you're not even thinking about another reality of what it would be like if you weren't with your current partner, you're not even considering what it would be like if you had a different lifestyle in a different place with someone else. Only then will you be totally present and capable of achieving fulfillment.

For some people, true commitment is hard. *Well, I love this person, but I really wish they were different in this way and that way.* No, if you make the commitment to a relationship and to a person, to make it work you need to accept and embrace your partner for who they are. If part of you wants your partner to change, you are not accepting them for who they are. If you're not accepting your partner for who they are, you will not have the connection you want. You will not have the relationship you want. You will not be able to go very far. It will limit you, and you certainly will not have a Radical Marriage.

The cool part is that 100% commitment is a choice. It's something you can absolutely find in your life. This is not to say that people are perfect, far from it. And that's okay. We can judge that our partner is imperfect and still be 100% committed and embrace their imperfection. We have a word for imperfections. We call them quirks. They are things about your partner that might bug you that you can accept and embrace if you choose to.

For example, David and Darlene have very different driving styles. Like most people, David drives a bit over the speed limit while Darlene is a "rule-follower" who respects the posted limit. This could easily turn into a conflict with either of them nagging the other to drive differently. But they respect each other's "quirk" and allow each other to have their individual styles. The point here is that when you're in a *Radical Marriage* you might not always agree, you might not always like it, but you can still embrace your partner fully for who they are. You don't try to change them and you don't reject certain parts of them. That's *Radical Commitment*.

Committing to Your Partner's Happiness

In today's immediate gratification, "Me, Me, Me" culture, we tend to focus on our *own* needs and our *own* happiness. In a Radical Marriage, you prioritize *your partner's* happiness. It doesn't mean you're being codependent and giving up your own happiness; it just means that you have a symbiotic relationship. If you and your partner want to be happy together and have a Radical Marriage, it is essential that you prioritize each other's happiness. It's also fantastic.

Imagine this:
You have a partner who is committed to your happiness.

Imagine this: You have a partner who is *committed* to your happiness. They want you to be happy. They put energy and priority into you being happy. Wouldn't you love to have that kind of partner? Wouldn't your life be great if you had somebody that was committed and devoted to your happiness? Well, you *can* have that. But first, you need to be committed to *their* happiness.

Let's say you have a 60/40 split, where you prioritize your partner's happiness 60% and your own happiness 40%. It's not that you're giving yourself up and that you don't care about your own happiness—certainly you will pursue having your needs met—but you are just prioritizing the relationship and your partner's happiness. Remember, we are talking about *Radical Marriage*, which requires *Radical Commitment*, which requires prioritizing your partner's happiness, which takes you beyond *good*, which takes you *beyond* happily ever after.

Is Lifelong Commitment Even Possible?

44% of people in their 20's believe that marriage is obsolete.

While it's clear the role of commitment is huge, there remains a lot of confusion about what commitment is. The marriage rate today is 51%, its lowest point. The divorce rate, however, remains at around 40-50%. In other words, despite the fact that there are fewer marriages, half of all marriages still end in divorce. What's more, the attitude toward marriage and commitment in young people is also at its lowest. In fact, a recent survey showed that 44% of people in their 20's believe that marriage is obsolete.

What is going on here?

For starters, in the past thirty years, cohabitation has increased by over 1,200%. It has become the most popular Step 2 in relationships. So, Step 1 is to find somebody and date a few times, and then it's, BOOM, Step 2, move in together. The problem is that moving in together is not *actual* commitment. It may look like commitment, and you may act like it's commitment, but it's not commitment. The reality is that, although there are exceptions, it generally doesn't work. In fact, the failure rate of cohabitation is over 80%. And no wonder. If your mindset is— *Well, if it doesn't work I can always leave*, this is the opposite of commitment. It's clear that what we are doing in relationships today is just not working.

Some time ago David published an article titled *What is Commitment in Relationships?* In it, he explored this question in great detail. Now, David has published a lot of things throughout his life and career. He has published many books and articles. He has published multiple websites for singles and couples. It's what he does. He's quite passionate about it and rather prolific at his work. But this one article—*What is Commitment in Relationships*—is without question the most popular article he's ever written. It's been clicked through and read by tens of thousands of people all over the world.

Is lifelong commitment even possible?

This tells you that the concept and question of commitment in relationships resonates with people who are struggling. And although they see commitment as important and seem to want it, there is a lot of skepticism and cynicism that also leaves them wondering, *Is lifelong commitment even possible?*

Personally, we believe that lifelong commitment is possible. But to make it work, we also believe that you first have to practice *Conscious Dating.* This means that we have to be clear about who we are and what we want and find a person who is aligned with that. Here's what's interesting, though: Even if it is a square peg in a round hole, research shows that you can make it work with *Radical Commitment.*

Research on Marriage

Committed relationships tend to be successful and fulfilling, even when the couple is unhappy

Research on marriage and commitment shows that *committed* relationships tend to be successful and fulfilling, even when the couple is unhappy. In fact, one of the most surprising research statistics we've stumbled across over the years is in the book, *The Case for Marriage,* by Maggie Gallagher and Linda Waite.

In this book there is a study that was done to track thousands of unhappily married couples. It was basically a series of simple survey questions: *Are you happy? Are you unhappy? Are you very happy? Are you very unhappy?* They identified unhappily married couples and then, five years later, asked them the same questions: *What's the deal? How are you feeling now?*

Guess what? Of the unhappily married couples who were still together five years later, two-thirds reported being happy. 67%! That blew us away. In their book, the authors called it the *Marital Endurance Ethic,* demonstrating that if you endure an unhappy marriage long enough, you have a good chance of being happy five years later.

Things change. Nothing stays the same.

There needs to be more research about this, but it's an intriguing and logical idea. Things change. Nothing stays the same. If you are unhappy today, even if it seems like it's an unsolvable problem that you can't live with, if you hang around long enough, chances are it will change. So the questions we have for you are, *How committed are you? Can you hang around long enough? What will you do in your relationship while you're sticking it out and trying to deal with an unsolvable problem?*

Beyond Happily Ever After

From a relationship coaching perspective, the concept of commitment is fascinating enough. But it also directly correlates to our personal relationship journey. Like Jack and Jill, these authors met and fell in love. We got married and seven years later were enjoying the most incredible life and relationship that we had ever experienced, far beyond what we had dreamed. Then another intriguing idea occurred to us: *What's next?* We had achieved and were already enjoying life happily ever after. *Now what?* Again, things don't stay the same. Things evolve. Things grow. It's passion evolution. It's in this spirit that we realized there is such a thing as *beyond* happily ever after.

But let's say you are successful in reaching your goal.
Then what?

Happily ever after is what we dream of when we haven't yet attained it. It's the vision of what we want our life and relationship to look like, someday, off in the distant future. Naturally, we figure we'll be happy when we get there. But let's say you are successful in reaching your goal. Then what? Is that it? Do you stop?

No!

You keep on going. You build on that. You take your relationship, in its current state of happily ever after, to a place we call *beyond* happily ever after. It's there that you will find yourself in a Radical Marriage. To have a *Radical Marriage*, you must be *radically committed*, because commitment, as research suggests, is an essential ingredient to a lasting successful relationship.

If you are not committed, you open the door to failure, and your relationship will eventually bomb. But if you stay committed, and you stick it out long enough, even if you are unhappy, the odds are in your favor that you'll end up happy. Of course, it helps to work on it as well, which you have already demonstrated a willingness to do since you are reading this book in the first place.

If commitment is the glue, if commitment is the secret sauce, if commitment is the key to making a lasting relationship be good or great, then *Radical Commitment* is the key to a *Radical Marriage*. Here, in the pages that follow, we have identified what Radical Commitment looks like. We have identified specifically what you can do to be committed in such a way that you can have a *radical relationship* and a *Radical Marriage*.

Commitment Defined

Commitment means you don't have an exit strategy.

Commitment means there are no exits. You are all-in. There is no part of you, no matter how small, that's holding back, thinking, *Well, if it doesn't work out, I can always leave.* No, commitment means you don't have an exit strategy. There is no escape hatch at the ready. Having said that, and though it may be intuitive to some people, there remains a lot of confusion about commitment.

That's why David's article "What is Commitment in Relationships?" is so popular. In our business we often encounter couples who are confused about commitment, but don't *know* they are confused. When David was a practicing therapist, it would happen on a regular basis.

Here's an example:

One day a couple came into David's office and sat down on his couch. The guy, who was very high energy, leaned forward and said in a Texas drawl, "We've been dating for three months now and we're real committed!"

"Okay," David said. Meanwhile, he looked over at the female partner who was subtly shaking her head and rolling her eyes, as if to say, "Well, maybe *he's* committed. But I'm not so sure." So, the guy had built up the commitment in his own head, but she hadn't bought it. That's not a committed relationship.

As a couple's therapist, David would need to know the relationship status to best serve his clients. If it wasn't offered up voluntarily and they weren't clearly married, he would have to ask: "Are you married? Are you engaged to be married? Are you thinking about it? Where are you as a couple?" He would follow that up with, "Are you in a committed relationship?"

Pop Quiz: What percentage of couples do you think said "Yes, we are in a committed relationship"?

Answer: 100%.

That's right, 100% of unmarried couples that came into David's office, when asked if they were in a committed relationship, said "yes," regardless of their situation, regardless of what their body language might have been revealing.

In their mind they were committed—even if it required some self-convincing to believe. The intent was there, as going to see a therapist does signify that they want to work on it, and does demonstrate a certain *level* of commitment, but it's not full-blown commitment. Over many years of seeing clients like this and further exploring what commitment is, David saw a need to define commitment for couples who *think* they're committed or are confused about commitment, which is really part of why their life and relationship aren't working out. Here's an excerpt from his article *What is Commitment in Relationships*:

In My Opinion, You Are *Not* In a Committed Relationship If ...

1. Your partner is not aware your relationship is committed

2. You are wondering if your relationship is committed

3. You and your partner have differences of opinion about the status of your relationship

4. Your friends and your family have different perceptions about the status of your relationship

5. You and your partner have not acted to explicitly formalize your commitment in some way

6. You are relying on verbal promises without a significant track record of them being kept

Promise vs. Commitment

It's worth noting that there's a difference between a promise and a commitment. A promise is something you say. It's something you intend. A commitment, however, is an act that keeps on going. It's something you do.

As an example, David was working with a woman who sought him out because she wanted a reality check. She said that her boyfriend cheated on her. Turns out, they had a long distance relationship. They had been together for six months and they saw each other on weekends. He ended up sleeping with somebody else.

David asked her the question, "Well, did you guys have a commitment?" She said, "Well, you know, we never really talked about it, but he was my boyfriend. He cheated on me."

Essentially, they were a dating couple, long distance, who hung out for six months on the weekends. They never talked about their relationship. They never made any commitments. They never even made any promises. But in her mind they were committed. Obviously, he wasn't.

Commitment is serious. It is something you can see. It is enforceable. It is an event. If you tell me you're committed and I ask you, "Oh, well when did that happen?" you should be able to tell me when and where and how. Even if it was on the top of the mountain with you and your partner in front of your God and nobody else was there, you should be able to tell me the day, the time, and the place. If you didn't explicitly formalize your commitment then how committed are you? You're merely committed in your mind. A true commitment is formal and there are absolutely no exits from it—not without serious consequences.

A commitment in a relationship is infinite.
It doesn't have an end.

A commitment in a relationship is infinite. It doesn't have an end. People don't commit to being married for five years. When we say "I do" we mean for life. It's part of who we are. It's in our DNA. If you ask people, "Would you prefer a temporary relationship or a permanent relationship with commitment?" and "When you get married, do you want to be married for a limited amount of time or for the rest of your life?" most people will tell you that they A) want commitment and B) want to grow old with the love of their life.

Of course there are cynics and "realists" to throw into the equation. They will argue that in reality, the divorce rate is high. In reality, relationships fail. In reality, commitment is an iffy proposition. All of that is true, but that's no reason to dismiss marriage. *Commitment* is what makes a relationship extraordinary and allows a couple to achieve higher levels of fulfillment and happiness than is possible without commitment. Commitment makes it safe, and we need emotional safety to truly experience love—to receive love and give love. True commitment says, "I'm not going anywhere. You are safe with me."

Pre-Commitment

In a relationship, there is a transition from dating to being a couple, and that transition happens when you both decide to be exclusive. The woman whose boyfriend "cheated" on her never had that assurance from him. They didn't agree to be exclusive. When you decide to be an exclusive couple where you're not dating anybody else, but you're not yet committed, you have reached the stage of a relationship we call pre-commitment.

Conscious couples in this important stage are thinking, *Is this the right relationship for me? Should I make a commitment here?* Again, most people want a commitment. They don't want to hang out in this stage forever, though sometimes they do, or think they do. Then, five or ten years later, they want more. The pre-commitment stage is an important stage where you can explore whether a relationship is right for you before making a commitment you might not be able to keep.

If at this stage you determine that it's not the relationship for you, if it doesn't fit everything that you're looking for, if you can't in good conscience live happily ever after with this partner, then it's probably best to move on and find something that is a better fit for both of you, because it's the best move in the long run.

It all depends upon what you're looking for. If you want happiness and fulfillment, and you realize there has to be a good fit for that to be sustainable and successful over time, then you'll say "no" to what you don't want and to what's *not* a good fit so that you can find what *is* a good fit for you.

In marriage, you make a lifetime commitment, though many married couples are not committed emotionally. When you settle, despite making a commitment to a particular partner, you let go of what you really want and you never forget what you really want. What you want is still a part of who you are so you are continually making sacrifices. There are needs and wants that are not going to happen. Some of those things are solvable, some you can get creative about. Some things you can let go of and others you can't.

We tend not to believe that we can have everything we want so we settle for what we have.

As responsible, mature adults we tend not to believe that we can have everything we want so we settle for what we have. We try to be *happy* with what we have. We're here to tell you it is absolutely possible to be ecstatically happy with what you have—but you have to be willing to let go of what you don't have. Many people in the world are frustrated because they are consciously or unconsciously not letting go of something, whether it's their first boyfriend who they never quite got over, or something else.

Here's an example: David loves boats—sailboats in particular. He loves the water. He is most happy being on, in, under, or near the water. Having a boat is just part of who David is. It makes him happy. If he doesn't have a boat, then he's not happy. It would be his dream to live on a boat.

David is married to the most wonderful woman in the world, Darlene, who makes him very happy, even without a boat. But these authors have a Radical Marriage. Darlene, who gets violently seasick, encouraged David to get a boat and made it her mission to conquer her motion sickness. In return, David does everything in his power to make being on the boat comfortable for Darlene (at this writing, so far so good) and they enjoy their boat as their "second home." There's even talk about living on a houseboat someday.

We all have concessions to make. We all make sacrifices. We all need to let go of some things that we might want to be with a particular person. And we can consciously be happy with that or we can unconsciously never let go of what we sacrificed. We can decide to be happy and stay in the moment, or we can tolerate our relationship day to day, staying in touch with how it isn't what we really want, always slightly aware of how our life is not the way we really want it to be.

Commitment is a choice.
It starts with accepting fully what you have...

Commitment is a choice. It starts with accepting *fully* what you have in your relationship and your partner, and letting go of the exits, including pining for what you don't have. As a way of accomplishing this and making it real, we have created *five promises*, specifically designed to help you achieve *Radical Commitment*—even if what you have isn't everything you've ever wanted in your life.

Five Promises of Radical Commitment

The First Promise: I promise to love you every day

Love is a choice. We get busy, we have moods, and we get frustrated. But if you are truly committed to your partner, you will choose to love them fully every day—even when you're mad at them, even when you're having a bad day. This is similar to *unconditional* love, but this is something more. This is actively making the choice: *I promise to love you every day.*

How many couples are living day to day where a partner gets irritated when her husband leaves his socks on the floor? She's nagged him and nagged him and nagged him. He's promised and promised and promised. It has reached the point where she is resentful and upset and she finds it hard to love him. She finds it hard to accept him for who he is, because 20 years later he still leaves his damn socks on the floor!

What she might do is promise to love him every day, even when he leaves his socks on the floor, which is a big shift for people. Many people can't do it. They can't let go of anger and resentment and judgment and the need for their partner to be different.

So promise number one is *I promise to love you every day.* Love is a choice. You choose to make that choice, always and every day.

The Second Promise: I promise to choose you first

Here you make your partner the most important person in your life and you do not take them for granted. You don't put anything else above them—not work, not home, not family, friends, kids, hobbies, nothing. You put your partner first, always.

Loving relationships are inclusive, not either/or.

For a lot of people, this scares them to death. *Huh? How can I possibly do that? What about my kids? What about my faith? What about this? What about that?* Choosing your partner first doesn't mean you are not prioritizing your family or anyone or anything else. Loving relationships are inclusive, not either/or.

Here's an example; when you travel by air the flight attendant runs through a series of safety instructions before taking off, one of which is, in case of a loss of cabin pressure, to put your mask on first, then assist your child. This is not a self-centered act, it's because you can't be present or help or be responsible for someone else if you're struggling yourself.

Your family and your kids will be much happier and better off if you're a solid team and have a strong couple partnership. To make that happen, you must choose your partner first. If you put your kids first, you have a kid-centered household and that tends to not work very well. The kids get spoiled and suck the oxygen from the marriage (to continue the air travel analogy) and your partner gets resentful because you end up living parallel lives. Choosing your partner first, always, above everything, is a form of *Radical Commitment*.

This can be especially tough for women. For them, it's important to note that it's not a matter of choosing the man over the child. It's a matter of prioritizing the relationship and the partner. To choose the man over the child is either/or. The goal here, if you are true partners, is to be a team and in this together. If your partner is choosing you first as well, they will support your priorities and goals and together you will be a strong team (and as they say, "there's no "*i*" in team").

In a successful, loving, committed relationship,
everything must happen in connection.

One of David's relationship mentors made a blanket statement some years ago that blew him away. He tried to find holes in it and to this day he can't. She said, "In a successful, loving, committed relationship, everything must happen in connection."

David said, "Everything?"

She said, "Everything."

Everything must happen in connection with *Radical Commitment* and in a *Radical Marriage*.

The Third Promise: I promise to take responsibility

Here is where you understand that your outcomes are 100% dependent upon your own choices and actions. You understand that your thoughts and feelings are your own. If you take 100% responsibility for your life, for your relationship, and for your family, you won't blame your partner when it's not working. You won't put responsibility on your partner to make it work. You will take responsibility for working with your partner to make it work. And, yes, you are going to choose your partner first, and you are going to choose to be in connection with them about your family and everything else.

Your "Experience"

There is this thing that happens inside your body and your mind we call your "experience." It is your thoughts and your feelings and your physical sensations. And guess what? It's all yours. It's unique to you. Everybody else in the world has their own experience, too. There is the subjective world, which is inside you, and there is the objective world, which is outside you. There is fact, which is measurable and observable and outside you, and there is opinion or judgment, which are the things you make up in your head. Relationships and life go smoother when we are aware of the difference.

When you have an opinion or a need or a judgment, that's all about you.

When you have an opinion or a need or a judgment, that's all about you. A sock-free floor, for example, is a subjective need. "I need you to pick up your socks. I don't want to pick up your socks. I judge that if you leave your socks on the floor you're sloppy." That's all about you. It's inside you, and if you can understand and own that, it's easier to love your partner, even when he leaves his socks on the floor.

Because, you know what? It's a completely valid form of existence. There are people that leave their socks on the floor and there are people that don't leave their socks on the floor. Both of them are okay. That's taking responsibility. And when we take responsibility for our own thoughts and feelings, wants and needs, judgments and opinions, we acknowledge that it's okay for other people to be different. That's *Radical Commitment*.

Avoiding responsibility boils down to blame and judgment. If we are judging somebody for being wrong or bad, then we are not taking responsibility for our own reality. Short of murder or other horrendous acts or crimes, nobody is objectively wrong or bad. That's reality. Taking responsibility means taking things out of the realm of right or wrong, good or bad, and accepting your partner for who they are. It's also being able to accept and love yourself for who you are.

The good news is that you don't have to take responsibility for other people's experience.

The most freeing experience of David's life came as an adolescent when he realized, *Hey, my parents are unhappy and it's not my fault … it's not about me!* You, too, will benefit greatly when you accept that in life there is what you are responsible for, that which is inside you, and there is what you are not responsible for, that which is inside others. Yes, you need to take full responsibility for who you are and what's inside you, but the good news is that you don't have to take responsibility for other people's experience. You can't, even if you wanted to, because that belongs to them.

Taking responsibility for your own experience is freeing, but for a lot of people, it's also scary. It can be scary to think that if your partner is not responsible for making you happy, that means,

OMG, I'm responsible for my own happiness! For many people this is the scariest thing in the world, so they hold onto making their partner right or wrong and they stay in judgment, because it is scary and unsafe for them to take full responsibility.

Men, especially, often feel like they need to make women happy. It's hardwired in them and it's a challenge to let go of that. But there's always going to be an internal struggle about something, man or woman. As part of our evolution, the struggles become about higher-order things. We no longer struggle with *Should I leave my family vulnerable to predators to go hunting*? Now we struggle with, *My partner's having a bad day. This isn't about me, is it?*

Being there, being compassionate, and being empathic means that you're not taking it all on. You're not taking on the blame or the responsibility and you're not trying to fix it. That way you can be fully present and supportive and compassionate. And that's what your partner really needs.

So if you are feeling responsible for your partner's happiness, it's time to work hard to let go of that and be present with compassion and empathy because that's how you're going to win. That's what your partner really needs. And that's how you will remain committed and fulfilled as a couple.

The Fourth Promise: I promise to say "Yes"

This is another promise that scares people, and it's one of our favorites: *I promise to say "Yes."* It's not just "Yes" sometimes. It's not just "Yes" when I feel like it or agree. It's "Yes" *always*.

---

*It's hard to be positively received
when somebody's saying "No" to you.*

Think about it: What do *you* want as a person? You want to be positively received, right? And it's hard to be positively received when somebody's saying "No" to you. You want a positive response. A relationship works best when you respond positively to your partner and your partner to you. This doesn't mean that you need to say "yes" to what does not work for you or what you can't do. That's not what this means at all. However, it does mean you don't say "no." So how do you say "yes" to something that you can't do or don't want to do? Simple: You find something that you *can* say "yes" to. Instead of saying "No, I can't because ..." you say, "Well, how about this ..."

Let's say your partner is *in the mood* and you're not. You're not feeling well. You have the classic headache. Rather than saying, "Not tonight dear, I have a headache" you might say, "You know what, I have a headache. How about in the morning?" You are positively receiving your partner's advances. You are saying *what* you can do and *when* you can do it. You are saying "Yes." You are not saying "yes" to having sex right now, because you have a headache. You are saying "yes" to having sex in the morning when you anticipate feeling better.

I promise to say "Yes" is responding positively to your partner all the time, every time. Instead of saying "no," you simply let them know what you can say "yes" to, and when. When this happens it creates safety. Remember: We need emotional safety to love and be loved and experience intimacy and fulfillment. If we know that we are going to be positively received, if we know that we are not going to be judged wrong or bad, we feel safe. And that is a wonderful feeling.

The Third Option

Let's say your partner says, "I'd like us to have another lover." Well, there are a lot of things—and that's one of them—that you might not imagine you could ever say "yes" to. But let's put aside your initial negative response, which, remember, is all about you and your judgment. If you are promising to choose your partner first, and you are promising to love them every day and you are taking responsibility for your own experience, including your judgments, including your repulsion about multiple lovers, then what *can* you say "yes" to?

60

Now, addressing this hypothetically, we don't know the answer, but there is a wonderful concept in a relationship that we call the *third option*. It states that in relationships it doesn't have to be a matter of black or white, his way or her way. There is always an alternative, and part of the adventure in life and in a relationship is being able to find that third option.

There is always a third option.

We don't need to speculate exactly what the third option might be for this hypothetical couple, one of whom wants to take on a lover. The important thing is, rather than responding with an emphatic "NO!", that the partner responds with an open-minded "yes" attitude such as "Hmmm, interesting, what do you have in mind about how that would work?" They might explore why that person wants to take on a lover, and on and on. In principle, though, there is always a third option, and when you promise to say "yes," you are committing to finding the third option. You're not necessarily saying "yes" to polygamy or polyamory or affairs, but wouldn't that be an adventurous and creative conversation to find the third option that fits that scenario? And we don't mean settling or sacrificing. We mean finding a creative solution that truly meets the needs of both partners, 100%.

The Fifth Promise: I promise to be your hero

Life is challenging. Our journey is full of struggle and we all need a hero. Our partner, the person who loves us the most, who knows us the best, who we have a lifelong committed relationship with, needs to be that hero. They need to be our champion, our primary supporter, somebody who will be there for us 100%, unconditionally, no matter what. It's that kind of safety and support that is needed for *Radical Commitment*.

Being your partner's hero means that you show up when they need you, no matter what. Even if it's scary for you, even if you feel out of your league and over your head, even if you feel helpless, even if you disagree with what they're doing, even if everyone else is criticizing them, you will still support them, advocate for them, and show up for them. They don't need to "earn" your support; they deserve your support simply because you're in a committed relationship. You promise to be their hero, no matter what.

This concept goes back to being babies and feeling dependent and secure when our parents are there, meeting our needs. Feelings of insecurity start happening when our parents aren't on top of our needs and we end up crying for an hour because we're hungry. It is soothing and creates emotional safety when you really know that your partner is there for you 100%. They promise to show up and be your hero.

Challenge Yourself

Each of these promises, when taken together, create *Radical Commitment*. They are also a stretch. They require effort. They are not easy. They are not automatic. This is what a conscious and radical relationship is all about. It's about making intentional choices that are unique in that they maximize your fulfillment as a couple.

The more you do it, the easier it will be.

Still, many people look at these promises and say, "I can't do that." They make this choice because they are scared. But our promise to you is that you can absolutely do every one of them. It's like exercise. The more you do it, the easier it will be. You just need practice and discipline.

Choosing to love your partner even when you are mad at them or disagree with them; choosing to put your partner first, even when you feel pulled by your kids; taking responsibility, even when you're sure it's your partner's fault that you're feeling the way you're feeling; finding something to say "yes" to, even when you're not in the mood and it just would be so much easier to say "no";

and being a hero, even when it's hard, and you're not feeling up to it or when you're feeling like your partner doesn't deserve it—all of these things are stretches. They are not easy. They take effort.

They are not automatic. They are conscious choices. And they will absolutely result in *Radical Commitment*, an essential ingredient of a *radical relationship* and of a *Radical Marriage*.

Summary of the Five Promises of Radical Commitment

1. I promise to love you every day
2. I promise to choose you first
3. I promise to take responsibility
4. I promise to say "Yes"
5. I promise to be your hero

Giving Your Partner the Gift of Radical Commitment

To allow you to immediately take action toward *Radical Commitment*, we have created a beautiful certificate you can download, print out, sign, and give to your partner. We believe that saying, "I make these five promises to you" is the best gift you could ever give your partner and your relationship, and it costs nothing. The promises are all in "I" language. They each refer to you and what you are going to do and what your choices are. This is not something that you discuss and negotiate. This is something that you promise your partner unilaterally. You are not expecting anything in return. You are not saying, "I will make these promises if you make these promises, too." It doesn't work like that.

Radical Action:

Our suggestion, if these five promises resonate for you, is to go to **www.radicalmarriage.com/5promises** and download and print out the certificate. Then sign it and give it to your partner and say, "Honey, I make these five promises to you." See if it resonates for your partner and see if your partner wants to reciprocate. But don't wait for approval. That's part of taking responsibility. *Radical Commitment* starts with you.

Chapter Three: Radical Communication
Part 1- The Communication Map

It's hard to consider marriage or any relationship without also thinking of communication. In terms of Radical Marriage, you will limit your possibilities unless you can refine your skills, improve your ability to handle differences and conflict, and challenge your relationship by harnessing the power of *Radical Communication*.

Through all of our study, experience and development, there remains a go-to method that can get you out of a communication jam, improve your couple relationship, and help you reach your level of desired fulfillment. It's something we call the Communication Map.

The Communication Map is a one–page communication system for all relationships. It's a tool David developed in his practice as a strategy to help couples with their communication, in a way they can relate to, without jargon, and that helps their situation and functioning immediately. It was designed so people could learn it in one hour or less and then go home and use it effectively and independently. At the time of its inception, no other communication model in existence could meet this criteria. So, David experimented, tested, and revised the process until the Communication Map came together as you see it today.

Many cope with conflict by avoiding it.

The Communication Map doesn't address feelings or the past. It was developed with the assumption that you must survive before you can thrive. As such, our priority with couples is "functioning first." Many couples get stuck in conflict around the big and little issues in their life. Nobody likes arguing, which causes bad feelings, and many cope with conflict by avoiding it, which causes resentment and hinders the relationship.

The Communication Map is a foundational system that provides a structure for effectively addressing issues and problems in any relationship. Couples can then use other skills to address feelings, reasons and motivations, the past, and other aspects that might enhance the relationship beyond solving problems.

The Communication Map was developed over two decades ago, and since that time we've heard from many, many people who like it. It's easy to learn, and it's universal enough to use in any relationship, including parent/child, manager/employee, friends, neighbors, and so on—while also allowing enough creativity for those seeking to go beyond happily ever after. People are often amazed that they can review a short tutorial (included below) and then effectively use the Communication Map right away, making their life immediately more functional and harmonious. We hope this will also be true for you and your partner as you explore *Radical Communication* as part of your *Radical Marriage*.

Getting Started with The Communication Map

The Communication Map illustrates what happens in communication and what to do about it when there is an issue in a relationship. The following graphic goes hand in hand with our Top Five Communication Tips for Couples, which will be discussed in more detail later in this chapter.

The Communication Map provides structure to promote safety and effective communication when you're experiencing a problem in a relationship, which is the highest risk time for unproductive conflict. Structure is of utmost importance. When you have a structure to follow and you know what to do and what not to do, then your communication and your relationship is far more productive. The Communication Map follows the 80/20 rule— about 80% is consciousness and understanding what's going on, and about 20% is what to do and what to say. The idea is fairly simple. The more complicated thing is being clear about how it works and what not to do.

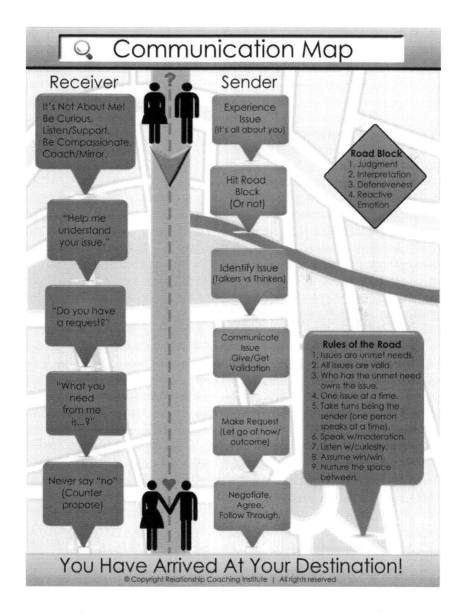

The Communication Map can be used in all settings. Here we apply it in the context of a Radical Marriage, but it is an applicable system for *all* relationships. And even though these tips are for couples, you can absolutely apply them to other areas of your life. In terms of developing a *radical relationship*, the Communication Map comes into play when one person experiences an issue or problem and needs to talk to the other person about it.

You must make sure the time and place
is conducive to good communication,
otherwise it won't work from the start.

Before you start communicating about an issue it's helpful to <u>make an appointment</u> or ask your partner if it's a good time for them. For example, "*I have something important to discuss. Is now a good time for you?*" Giving your partner a heads-up allows them time and opportunity to prepare and clear their head to listen and be receptive. In addition to making sure it's a good time to talk, it helps to go to a <u>private space</u>, free from distractions. You must make sure the time and place is conducive to good communication, otherwise it won't work from the start.

Once you have found a suitable environment, you can employ the system, which we will delve into now.

Nine Rules of the Road

Rule of the Road Number One: Issues are Unmet Needs

If it weren't a need, it wouldn't be an issue.

In any communication there is a sender and a receiver. An exchange is forthcoming when the sender is experiencing an issue of some kind and needs to communicate about it to the receiver. This happens through a specific process that we will detail shortly. For now, it's enough to assume that your partner isn't complaining about something trivial or fabricating something to bug you about. We must assume that any problem or issue in a relationship boils down to an unmet need. If it weren't a need, it wouldn't be an issue.

Rule of the Road Number Two: All Issues are Valid

If we assume that *all* issues are valid then we won't argue with each other about the validity of the issue. It is not nice nor is it productive to discount somebody's issue. *"Oh, come on now, that's no big deal. What's your problem? Don't be ridiculous."* Don't allow someone to discount your issue and don't discount their issue. Just the fact that you experience an issue makes it valid. You don't need to justify it or get agreement about whether it's an issue or not. All issues, big and small, are valid.

To go even further, if you are committed to your partner's happiness you appreciate and welcome your partner's issues as road signs that make your job easier—*Here's exactly what I need to be happy!*

Rule of the Road Number Three: Who Has the Unmet Need, Owns the Issue

This is what we call David Steele's Law of Relationship, and it goes two ways. For the sender, it means that if you have an issue, it's about you, you own it. It's yours. It belongs to you. There is no universal issue about which you can say, *"Everybody* will have an issue with this." Some people will. Some people won't. Needs and issues are subjective, not facts. They are your truth, not necessarily a truth that others share.

If something is an issue for you, it means you have a need and that need is unmet. It's not automatically an indictment that your partner is in the wrong. For example, what if your partner comes home late and doesn't call? In some relationships that might be a problem; in others it might not be a big deal. If you have a need to know what to expect, it will be an issue for you if that need is unmet when your partner is late and doesn't call. The need is yours and the issue is yours. Your partner being late is a fact. It doesn't make them right or wrong. It doesn't make your issue less valid. It simply means you must take an attitude of ownership.

Taking ownership of your needs and issues in a relationship is important. It empowers you to be responsible for your needs and is much less likely to put your partner on the defensive, because you're not making them wrong or blaming them for your unmet need.

What this means for the receiver is that it's not about you. It's not your issue. Your job is to let the sender have their issue and to not try to take it away from them by having an issue with their issue. If you take their issue personally and make it about you then you will hit a road block. If, however, you let them have their issue and support them to get their need met, you will help yourself as well, giving you a happy relationship and a happy partner.

Rule of the Road Number Four: One Issue at a Time

When people talk about more than one issue at a time it often goes all over the place. They bring out everything and the kitchen sink—every resentment they've saved up and every little grievance. If you want to have productive communication and resolve something between you and your partner, you must focus on one thing at a time.

Rule of the Road Number Five: Take Turns Being the Sender—One Person Speaks at a Time

---

This is basic playground behavior: share and take turns.

This is basic playground behavior: share and take turns. If you don't, arguments happen. When one person prevents the other person from speaking, the other person feels the need to talk louder to be heard. And then it goes back and forth. So, take turns being the sender.

71

Granted, this technique is simple but not necessarily easy. When you're hitting a road block it feels so urgent to have your partner listen to you. As a result, you have a hard time being present. Being there for your partner and letting them speak their piece, uninterrupted, sometimes takes a heroically conscious effort—but it can be done.

Rule of the Road Number Six: Speak with Moderation

If you're taking turns, then you don't need to yell to be heard. You can speak with moderation. Productive communication is about being calm, respectful, and choosing your words carefully.

Rule of the Road Number Seven: Listen with Curiosity

How often are you thinking about what you are going to say while they are talking?

If you truly want to be an effective communicator, you must be curious about where your partner is coming from and not prejudge them as wrong. You must not speculate. *"Well, they really mean this."* or *"They're just saying that because of this."*

Look at your partner through new eyes. Listen to them as if you were listening to them for the first time. Listen with curiosity. When you do, you will learn something new about your partner and your relationship will not only work better, it will be more passionate and fulfilling.

Think about your patterns when listening to your partner: How often are you thinking about what you are going to say while they are talking? Sometimes we don't even give the other person a chance to finish before we insert our opinions. This is human nature and we all have this tendency, however, it's an unproductive bad habit. It takes effort to adopt an attitude of curiosity, but it will help you listen effectively.

This *Rule of the Road* is also part of taking turns. If your partner is the sender, then you need to be the receiver. You need to listen. If it's your turn to be the sender then you have a right to expect your partner to listen and receive you. If they are not playing that role you can request them to do so.

Rule of the Road Number Eight: Assume Win-Win

Most of us *intellectually* grasp the idea that we can negotiate and find a way that works for both of us. But often *unconsciously* there is an assumption that if you get your way then I'm not going to get my way. If you win then I lose. This scarcity mentality drives people into conflict. People who think like this don't trust that their needs will be met if their partner's needs are met at the same time. It's *either/or*. We like to believe that it is *both/and*. We assume the win–win, which if you follow the structure of The Communication Map, won't be a problem.

Rule of the Road Number Nine: Nurture the Space Between

Here's a concept that we often forget about, and many couples don't even know about. A relationship is more than just two people; there is a space between where your relationship lives. It's where your children and everyone else that comes into contact with you and your partner live. There's an emotional atmosphere between you and your partner and it needs to be clean in order to be fulfilled and happy. If you have unresolved conflict, if your communication is not open and effective, or if there are resentments, disappointments and unresolved issues between you and your partner, then it is going to pollute the space between you—and everyone, including you, will feel it.

Each partner is entirely responsible
for what happens in the space between.

Since the space between is the relationship, we want to nurture that space. We want to treat it as sacred. It's not just about your partner and it's not just about you. It's the combination of both of you, and you are both responsible for it, 100%, not 50/50. Each partner is entirely responsible for what happens in the space between.

Communication Map Step One: Experience the Issue

As we mentioned earlier, the sender is the one with the issue, and they play a critical role in communication. As the sender, "It's all about you," but let's talk about the role of the receiver for a moment.

Eighty percent of being a good receiver is attitude. It's being curious about what's going on for your partner. It's realizing, *Hey, it's not about me! My partner, whom I love and care about, has an issue. They have an unmet need and it's not necessarily my fault. Although I might have contributed to it, their issue originated and lives inside them, so I need to be compassionate, listen to what's going on, and support them.*

The best role for the receiver is that of a *coach*. The receiver should ask questions about what's going on for the sender and *mirror* back what he hears. Let's again take the example where one partner comes home from work late and didn't call. They usually come home at 5:00 p.m., but this evening they didn't get home until 7:00 p.m. No call, dinner is cold, and the partner that has been waiting and worrying is upset.

In this situation, when the receiver finally gets home, the sender might say, "Where have you been? I've been so worried. You are late and you didn't call and I'm really upset and you are a jerk and you're inconsiderate and I can't believe you didn't call me. Dinner's cold and it's all your fault!"

Communication Map Step Two:
Experience Road Block (or not!)

Road Blocks involve one of four things:
judgment, interpretation, defensiveness, or reactive emotion.

The sender experienced an issue because the receiver was late, and the sender hit a road block. Road Blocks involve one of four things: judgment, interpretation, defensiveness, or reactive emotion.

Judgment means right or wrong, good or bad. *You are wrong and bad for being late.*

Interpretation is speculation, making meaning, or creating stories. In this case, it's around you being late or why you're late. "You are inconsiderate for being late and you must have something to hide otherwise you would have called to let me know that you were going to be late. You must be feeling guilty about something so that's why you didn't call."

Defensiveness is the other side of judgment. It's what happens when you're feeling attacked. It's a self-protective knee jerk. It would be understandable and common for the receiver in this situation to hit a road block, get defensive, and say, "What do you mean? It's only two hours. Dinner's not cold yet. This was just one time … my cell phone died. Give me a break."

Reactive emotion is feeling an emotion and acting upon it. We characterize the primary emotions as Mad, Sad, Glad, Fear, and Shame. All other emotions tend to be variations of these five primary emotions. When you experience an emotion, your nervous system is stimulated into fight or flight mode and it's much harder to communicate productively because it becomes about how you feel. Then you hit a road block, which is solid and you have nowhere to go. It's a dead end.

Hitting a road block disrupts the connection between you and your partner and the issue and unmet need cannot be addressed until you can back up and start over. The concept of road blocks is meant to help you understand what's going on. *Okay, I'm in judgment right now* or *I'm wrapped up in my interpretation of why you're doing this* or *I'm feeling defensive right now* or *I'm in a reactive emotion.* Once you're conscious enough to realize that you're up against a road block, you can give yourself a moment to recalibrate and get back on track.

Communication Map Step Three: Identify the Issue

There's a difference between experiencing something and being clear what it is you're experiencing.

If you're the sender and you're experiencing an issue, you must first clearly identify and communicate that issue. This is important for a simple yet profound reason: There's a difference between experiencing something and being clear what it is you're experiencing.

Often, you initially have a physical reaction accompanied by all sorts of thoughts and judgments. And while your general feeling of discomfort is clear to you, you're not necessarily clear about exactly what the problem is. If you're upset and you try to talk about the problem when you're not clear about it, it's not going to come out very pretty. Referring back to our example, if you're upset that your partner is late and you just ranted about it, you need to back away from the road block, identify specifically what your issue is and communicate it clearly to your partner.

Communication Map Step Four: Communicate the Issue

Talkers and Thinkers

Talkers tend to judge thinkers as too aloof and withdrawn.
Thinkers tend to judge talkers as too chatty and indirect.

There are two kinds of people in relationships: There are the *talkers* and the *thinkers*. The *talkers* need to talk about it first. They pretty much think out loud. They need to talk it out with their partner so they can get clear about what's going on for them. They need to express themselves to clearly formulate their issue.

The *thinkers* need to think about it first. They need to internally process so they can form the words and meaning and communicate that to their partner. If you try to get thinkers to talk too soon it's not going to come out very well and can lead to disaster. If you don't let talkers talk it out first and expect that what they say is going to be clear at the outset, you're asking for trouble.

To facilitate *Radical Communication*, you need to know whether you're a talker or a thinker, and whether your partner is a talker or a thinker, so you can satisfy each other's needs. Interestingly, couples often have one talker and one thinker. It's like we seek each other out for a complementary relationship. Nevertheless, processing things differently can present challenges in a relationship.

Talkers tend to judge thinkers as too aloof and withdrawn. Thinkers tend to judge talkers as too chatty and indirect. If you're the talker and your partner has an issue, it's going to be hard for you to let the thinker think, because you need to talk about it. If you're the thinker it's going to be hard for you to let your partner talk about it, because you need to process things internally and you automatically project that that's what they should do. You just want the bottom line. You wish that they would just be quiet and think about it first and then come to you when they have it all figured out and put into a reasonable presentation, but that's not the way it happens.

People almost always know what they are. If you ask somebody, "Are you a talker or a thinker?" they'll usually be able to answer with certainty. If they don't, it's very easy to find out—just ask their partner. A person almost always knows what their partner is. And it's amazing, if not stereotypical, how often the thinkers are the men and the talkers are the women.

Irrespective of gender, in identifying the issue and being able to communicate it, the sender needs to talk and the receiver needs to listen. Referring back to The Communication Map, this principle falls under *Receiver* as "Help me to understand your issue." This is particularly important to avoid confusion when you have a prejudged idea of the issue. Referring back to our example, the root of the problem may appear obvious: *I was late and I didn't call.* Seems pretty clear, right? But is it?

When you assume where your partner is coming from you don't give them room to express what they're really thinking and feeling. To improve communication we must curb our tendency to prejudge and presume and instead really listen with an open mind. We must show compassion, ask questions, and mirror back what we're getting. Again, the attitude is, "Help me understand your issue." We need to support our partner in identifying and communicating the issue clearly and specifically, even if we think we know what it is.

The solution becomes clear when the issue becomes clear.

The solution becomes clear when the issue becomes clear. If you try to solve something when you're not crystal clear about the problem, the solution won't work. This is especially hard for men.

They feel bad when their partner is unhappy and they want to fix it. They want to be the hero and jump in and save the day. What they really need to do is work hard to be patient and not take it personally. They need to let their partner own the issue, support them in communicating it, and offer ideas and solutions only if requested.

"Help me understand your issue"

Getting back to our example, let's say you're trying to support your partner in dealing with you being late. You could say, "I'm sorry I'm late and didn't call, dear, but please help me understand … what specifically is your issue with that?" Don't assume—unless your partner clearly says so—that being late and not calling is the issue.

Next, let's say the sender's response is "You're late, it's seven o'clock. You usually come home at five and you usually call if you're late, and you didn't call this time." Notice those are facts. Facts are typically inarguable, measurable events, but by themselves they don't identify an issue. As we mentioned before, what might be an issue for one person might be acceptable for another.

Starting with the facts is an excellent communication strategy, but then you must drill down a little deeper. You can mirror their response and say, "Yes, it's seven o'clock, I usually come home at five, and I didn't call." Then follow that up with a genuine attitude of curiosity by again asking, "What specifically about my being late is a problem for you?"

In this situation the sender might elaborate by saying, "Well, I was worried and I didn't know why you hadn't called." The receiver might listen to that and again mirror, "Okay, so it's seven o'clock and I'm late and I didn't call and you were worried. Do I understand your issue?"

Communication Map Step Five:
Confirm and Validate the Issue

It's easy to assume you understand what's going on, but at this point, maybe you do and maybe you don't. This is where you transition to step five in the Communication Map. You are seeking *confirmation* from the sender and getting a nod of the head—that positive, "Yes! That's my issue!" This allows you to reflect it back and give them *validation* of their issue.

The receiver might be surprised that what they thought was the issue was not really the issue.

In this case the sender might say, "You know what? It's not so much about you being late; it's that I cooked this wonderful dinner and it cost a lot of money and now it's cold. That's what I'm most upset about." Given this information, the receiver might be surprised that what they *thought* was the issue was not *really* the issue.

In conflict resolution, it's up to the sender to communicate the issue, and it's up to the receiver to help the sender communicate what it's really about. So, the receiver might mirror that back as "Oh, okay. You're saying what you're really upset about is you spent all this money on this great meal and now it's cold and you're disappointed and you're upset about that." If the sender responds, "Yes," then you know you have agreement, confirmation, and validation of what the issue is.

It started off as, "You're late, you jerk ... you're so inconsiderate." Now it's, "Well, I'm just really upset because I made this special meal and waited for you so we could enjoy it together, and now it's cold and I'm hungry and I wish you would have called."

To recap, the first hurdle, if you are the sender, is being clear about the issue. Then you need to make sure your partner understands it. You need to get and give validation about the real issue. Then you can focus on meeting the unmet need. This might sound obvious, but many couples skip this step and don't mirror or reflect their understanding at all. They just assume each knows what the other means.

Getting and giving confirmation means that the receiver reflects back their understanding of the issue to the satisfaction of the sender: "Yes, you've got it." And if the receiver isn't mirroring, the sender can ask, "Now, what's your understanding of my issue here?"

Once the issue is clear to both partners, the next step is for the sender to make a request. As tempting as it might be for the receiver to fix it or offer solutions, only the sender really knows what would meet their unmet need, so they need to ask for what they want. The receiver's role is to support the sender in making a request. If the receiver is too quick to give advice, they prevent the sender from taking responsibility and making a request.

Communication Map Step Six:
Make a Request

The alternatives to requesting are ineffective:
complaining, demanding, threatening, criticizing,
mind reading, or entitlement.

Requesting is the most important communication skill, period. We all have issues, we all have unmet needs, we all have things we want in a relationship for it to work for us. If we don't make a request, what are we going to do? The alternatives to requesting are ineffective: complaining, demanding, threatening, criticizing, mind reading, or entitlement.

Complaining: You're late, and now the expensive dinner that I spent hours preparing is ruined.

81

Demanding: You need to call if you're going to be late!

Threatening: You better call next time or else you're going to sleep on the couch!

Criticizing: What's the matter with you that you don't call if you're late? You're so inconsiderate!

Mind reading: You should know that I need you to call if you're going to be late!

Entitlement: I'm your wife and I worked hard to cook for you and I deserve a call if you're going to be late!

Strategies focused on the negative don't work very well. Requesting, the only productive option, focuses on the positive of what you need to make things work.

After the issue and unmet need is communicated in step four of the Communication Map, confirmed and validated in step five, it's time to move on to the solution. Here, the sender makes a request that will meet the unmet need, and if they don't, the receiver supports them to do so by asking "Do you have a request?"

Sometimes the sender gets so absorbed in getting the issue off their chest and feels so good talking about it that they have a hard time moving forward. Similarly, while a good receiver will let the sender fully express himself, if it goes on too long or becomes repetitive the receiver can support the sender by asking, "Do you have a request about that? How can I support you to get your need met in this situation?"

Let go of how

All that matters is that the need is met, not how it's met.

A need is interesting in that there are many ways to meet it. You can make a request, but it's a good idea to let go of the outcome, or, to let go of the *how*. Since there are many ways to meet a need all that matters is that the need *is* met, not *how* it's met. Your job is to come up with a way of meeting the need that works for both of you.

Sometimes couples get stuck here because they attach themselves to a particular outcome, a particular *way* of getting their need met. "I want you to call me by 4:50 if you're going to be late." That might not always be possible. Again, what matters is that your need *is* met, not *how* it's met.

Sometimes, after becoming clear about their issue, the sender decides they don't need anything different from the receiver. In this situation the sender might say, "You know, honey, I just realized that I did this to myself. I know you often have late meetings in the middle of the week and I probably shouldn't have gone all out like that tonight. I was in such a good mood and looking forward to seeing you tonight, and I got all excited when I saw your favorite dinner on sale today and wanted to cook you a special meal. I should have put it in the freezer until the weekend."

Incidentally, there are two possible responses to a request. The first is an unqualified, immediate agreement: "Yep, no problem, I can do that." The second option is a proposal of something that might work better for the receiver and still meet the need of the sender: "Well, I'd like to, but that won't work for me because of this, so, how about this?"

From decades of experience, we estimate that the first request doesn't work about 75% of the time. So, odds are, your first request is not going to be the win-win you're looking for. It's not going to be what works best and most effectively for both of you. You'll need to go to the next step, step seven in the Communication Map: Negotiate.

Communication Map Step Seven: Negotiate

In Chapter One we referred to compromise as a lose-lose situation. Here we want to go further and note the distinction between *compromise* and *negotiation*.

Compromise occurs when two people give up part of what works for them or what they need to meet somewhere in the middle. *Negotiation* is when both people get what they need and, therefore, are each 100% happy; they don't feel like they're giving up anything. It's a win-win, and it's worth the time and effort to come to an agreement.

Negotiation is a creative process whereby the sender and receiver take an issue, discuss it, brainstorm, and come up with an option that truly works for both parties. Often that option won't be apparent right away, so couples will dig in and focus on either/or. *"We're either going to solve it my way or your way."*

There's probably a creative solution out there someplace. You just have to find it.

Again, as we discussed with *Radical Commitment*, there is a *third option*. It's something that will be a unique reflection of both you and your partner and it doesn't always appear right away. It's worth brainstorming and being creative to find it. Ask friends and family for ideas. Do some research on the internet. Let it sit for a while. If you have an unsolvable problem, or something that *seems* unsolvable, just know that there's probably a creative solution out there someplace. You just have to find it.

Working to find the third option is worth it because if you come up with an agreement that doesn't really work for one of the parties, it's not going to stick. You want to come up with something that truly works for both parties, so it does stick. And if you don't know what it is right away don't worry about it; it will likely turn up eventually.

You Don't Know What You Don't Know

One of our favorite sayings is *You don't know what you don't know.* The implication is that you must be patient with yourself and be patient with the process. Your issue is not an emergency. In fact, with all of our experience working with couples we have yet to see a communication problem where 911 should be called. But it often feels urgent. We want to solve it right now, we are feeling bad right now, and we are attached to an idea right now. But if in this process the answer doesn't readily appear to you, be patient and agree on a plan for how you're going to find the solution together. *You don't know what you don't know.* Talk about it, think about it, get some ideas from family and friends, brainstorm, and be patient with the process.

If you're committed and you're not going anywhere, you'll at some point find a way to solve the problem.

If you're committed and you're not going anywhere, you'll at some point find a way to solve the problem. *"Well, you see the reason I'm late is because I was in a meeting, and I couldn't call you because I was in a meeting. When I got out of the meeting, you know, we only live five minutes away so it was going to take as much time to call you as it would just to drive home. I don't know what to do!"*

If you don't know what to do, talk about it, brainstorm some options, get creative and between the two of you a third option will eventually appear. If you're open-minded and looking for it, a good solution can be found.

"What you need from me is ...?"

Getting back to our example, we see that the issue wasn't really about being late. It was about needing some advance warning to hold off an expensive, wonderful dinner that the sender was preparing. You could brainstorm that. You could come up with the idea of text messaging, which wouldn't interfere with the meeting. Most cell phones even have pre-saved messages that say "running late" or "in a meeting," which can be sent quickly, easily, and unobtrusively in a few seconds.

The receiver's role in negotiating is to help the sender identify a solution that meets their need and that the receiver is able to do. If you are the receiver, realize that it's not about you. *Be curious, listen, support, be compassionate, and mirror* back with the intent to really understand what the sender's issue is. You can also *be a coach* by asking, *"Do you have a request?"* or *"What is it that you need from me?"* Help the sender communicate what it is they need and what would resolve the issue for them.

Never Say "No"

As a final suggestion for the receiver about requesting and negotiation, remember *The Fourth Promise* from the *Radical Commitment* chapter: *I promise to say "Yes."*

If your partner makes a request of you, stay positive.
Never say "no."

If your partner makes a request of you, stay positive. Never say "no." Instead of shooting down what doesn't work for you, *counter-propose* something that *would* work for you. From the sender's perspective, it doesn't feel good to be denied. *"Nope, sorry, can't do that."*

It is much more productive and loving to say, *"Well, honey, you know I'd really like to do that, but I'm not sure I can do it that way, so how about this?"* Suggest something that you can do that would meet their needs.

Communication Map Step Eight:
Agree

You can apply these strategies in all areas of your life. Taking it even further, you and your partner can make a pact with each other. Look at your partner, shake hands, and say, "Yes, we agree never to say 'No'!" It's a positive way of being in a relationship. It's being safe and trusting that your partner will receive you and listen to you, and be responsive to you when you have a request or a need or an issue and that they won't say "no" to you.

This can also be applied beyond your partner to everyone, especially your kids. Let's say your five-year-old sees a television commercial and then says *"Mommy, Mommy, can we go to Disneyland tomorrow?"* You could say *"No, you have school tomorrow."* Or, you might say, *"Disneyland would be a lot of fun. You know what? We're going to Disneyland this summer!"* Instead of saying "no" and concentrating on what you can't do and why you can't do it, how about responding with what you can do, when, where, and how?

This step in The Communication Map requires you to *agree* on a solution that truly works for both of you, one that meets the need of the sender and that the receiver gladly is able to do.

Communication Map Step Nine:
Follow Through

The final step of the Communication Map is to *follow through*. This is how you know it's a plan that works. It's how you know it's a commitment that will stick. Just as there is a distinction between negotiation and compromise, there is a distinction between a commitment and a promise.

A *promise* is when you make an *agreement* that you intend to keep. A *commitment* is where you actually *show up and do it*. A *promise* is a statement of *intent*, a kind of internal commitment that you fully intend to keep. A *commitment* involves *action*.

You might in all sincerity make a promise yet not be able to keep it, for a variety of reasons. Assuming positive intent of both parties, if you weren't able to keep the agreement, it's probably not your fault. More likely it was not a good agreement in the first place.

The definition of a good agreement in The Communication Map is one that you can keep because it works for both of you.

The definition of a good agreement in The Communication Map is one that you can keep because it works for both of you. But sometimes you won't know if it works until you give it a try. A good agreement is one that you can keep and that you want to keep because it's doable for you, you care about your partner, and you want them to be happy. If the follow-through doesn't happen the issue will repeat itself, and you must go back to the drawing board and come up with a plan that works for both of you.

We are Human

It's important to forgive each other for being human and to be patient with each other and with the process. The receiver must learn how to listen and learn how to not take it personally. The sender must learn how to be clear about what's going on for them, to recognize when they're hitting a road block, and to get back on track.

There is no such thing as perfection, so don't be too hard on yourself or your partner. What matters is your positive intent and applying The Communication Map as best you can toward a mutually beneficial solution. Just by understanding this process and practicing these steps over time, you'll find yourself bouncing back from road blocks sooner and sooner, until the day comes that you rarely, if ever, hit a road block.

Now, some couples do have hard-to-solve or unsolvable problems that require professional intervention, so if The Communication

Map isn't working for you with your best effort, it may be time to get some help.

Disclaimers aside, the Communication Map is pretty simple. It provides structure and takes something intangible and murky—words and hot air going back and forth—and makes it tangible and clear.

If you're the one with the issue or problem, you're the sender. Your goal is to identify and communicate your issue clearly and make a request about it.

If you're the receiver your job is to not take the sender's issue personally. You must support them to identify what it is and make a request about it.

Together, you can find a resolution that fits.

For most functional couples with basic communication skills and enough emotional maturity to manage their emotional reactivity and bounce back from road blocks, this is all that's needed. It will help you effectively address the spectrum of relationship issues and assist you in dealing with problems. It won't altogether prevent conflict, but it can help you handle conflict positively and effectively. By extension, it will enable you to further enjoy your life together and grow your love, trust, connection, and intimacy to *radical* levels.

You have a choice in how to handle any issue. As long as you have a choice you might as well choose what works and not repeat an unproductive pattern over and over, because behavior does follow patterns; nothing ever happens just once. When you make this choice, and you do it time and again, you'll develop the skill of being able to restore connection anytime.

Summary of Communication Map Steps

Step One: Experience the issue
Step Two: Hit road block (or not!)

Step Three: Identify the issue
Step Four: Communication the issue
Step Five: Confirm and validate the issue
Step Six: Make a request
Step Seven: Negotiate
Step Eight: Agree
Step Nine: Follow through

Top Five Communication Tips for Couples

In putting theory into practice, there are several things you can do:

Communication Tip Number One: The Three Magic Words of Listening

There are three magic words you can use when listening to somebody. Usually we want to insert what we think, but if you're listening with curiosity you'll say, "Is there more?" And when somebody says that to you, you usually say, "Well, yes, there is!" Asking "Is there more?" is contrary to what we usually do. Most of the time, when our partner says something, we want to quickly say what's on our mind about that. It is far more effective to just listen, take it in, and help your partner say even more about what's going on for them.

This process is like peeling away the layers of an onion, revealing more and more as you go. Your job as a listener is to wait until it's all out, and then respond to it. If you care about your partner and want a great relationship with them, you'll be a good listener and invite them to share all they need with you by asking them "Is there more?"

If you're wondering what the *three magic words of speaking* might be, here they are: "I love you." When you're upset at your partner and you have feelings and thoughts that are negative, it's always helpful to be in touch with and communicate: "You're my partner and *I love you*, but I'm really pissed right now."

Communication Tip Number Two: It's Not About You

Not taking it personally makes it easier to be the receiver.

In the art of communication, you need to remember "It's not about you." We covered this earlier in talking about The Communication Map but it bears repeating. If your partner is experiencing an issue, it's their issue and they own it. It's not about you. Don't take it personally. Not taking it personally makes it easier to be the receiver. "Okay, I love you and I want you to be happy. So tell me what's on your mind and we'll see how we can resolve this." If you take it personally, get defensive, and make it about you, you're not able to fully be there for your partner.

Communication Tip Number Three: It's All About You

The reason we're upset is about us,
not the situation or the behavior.

When we're upset about something it's human nature to direct our attention to the person who stimulated those feelings for us, as if it's their fault that we're upset. The truth is, in any given situation there are some people who would be upset about it and others who wouldn't. That means the reason we're upset is about us, not the situation or the behavior.

This scenario is a 90/10 formula: If you're upset about something, 90% of the emotional energy is related to the past and only 10% is in the present. Another helpful paradigm is to be clear about what are *facts, judgments, and feelings* and being able to distinguish them from each other. Separating them out allows for more objectivity and conscious choice.

Let's take our earlier example:

The facts are 1) you're late 2) you usually come home at 5:00 p.m., and 3) now it's 7:00 p.m. and you didn't call.

Judgments are opinions and interpretations like, "You're wrong" and "You're bad" and "You're inconsiderate" and "You're a jerk" and "You shouldn't do that."

Feelings are things like anger, anxiety, fear, and abandonment. When we confuse these things and bundle them all up in a diatribe, our communication doesn't work very well. "You're late, it's 7:00, you didn't call, dinner is ruined, that's the most inconsiderate thing that I've ever experienced in my life." This is simply reactive. Being conscious and separating the facts from the judgments and the feelings allows us to have more choices in how we respond to the situation and avoid hitting a road block.

Communication Tip Number Four: Turn Complaints into Requests

We have many needs.
It's impossible that they're all going to be met all of the time.

We mentioned that in our opinion *requesting* is the most important communication skill. We have many needs. It's impossible that they're all going to be met all of the time. When you have an unmet need and you experience an issue, you need to be able to make a request about that, respectfully, in connection with your partner. We need to create a win-win that does not make our partner wrong and bad. It's important that we approach this in a positive and productive manner, by requesting, instead of complaining, demanding, threatening, criticizing, mind reading, or with a sense of entitlement.

Communication Tip Number Five: Tell Your Truth

The *Rules of the Road* of the Communication Map are important. They create the kind of safety you need to be able to tell your truth, which is being authentic with your partner about your thoughts, feelings, needs, and wants. That is often scary for couples. It's a big risk to say what you're really thinking, feeling, needing, and wanting. But intimacy, which we will explore further in the next chapters, is what real connection and love is all about. And intimacy requires telling your truth.

The main reason people don't tell their truth to each other is that they fear conflict. They don't want to hurt or have an argument with their partner. They want everything to be okay, and they fear that if they tell the truth, that it's not going to be okay.

The Communication Map gives you a structure that allows you to express any issue and get your needs met. It doesn't have to be an argument, it doesn't have to be a conflict, and it doesn't have to feel bad. So, practice telling your truth, even if it's scary, because that's where true intimacy and connection comes from.

Summary of the Top Five Communication Tips for Radical Communication

1. The three magic words of listening – "Is there more?"
2. It's not about you
3. It's all about you
4. Turn complaints into requests
5. Tell your truth

Radical Action:

We suggest getting a laminated copy of the Communication Map from www.TheCommunicationMap.com and posting it in a visible spot in your home or office so that you can refer to it on the spur of the moment to remind you how to respond to potential situations of conflict. Keep it handy, and when you or your partner experience an issue, just grab it, put it in front of you, follow the structure, and within a few short minutes you'll be back in connection.

Use It Wisely

Our hope is that you will take The Communication Map and use it in all your relationships, especially your intimate relationships, so that from now on you will always have a way to reconnect when there is an unmet need and an issue. It's simple, effective, and practical. It's also foundational.

Remember, this is about functioning first. We need to survive before we can thrive. Once you have the survival part figured out, you can build on it and use it in more creative ways. The Communication Map will not only ensure your survival by helping you get your needs met and by bringing your communication to a functional level; it will allow you to then thrive and be happy, love more deeply and experience fulfillment, and seamlessly slide into the realm of *Radical Communication* as a building block for your *Radical Marriage*.

Chapter Four: Radical Communication
Part 2 - Experiencing Your Experience

With the foundation of resolving conflict under your belt, the stage has been set for more advanced strategies. Moving into the next phase, there are useful parameters for Radical Communication and they have to do with "experiencing your experience."

We can't be so rigid that we reject reality.

Despite being in a committed relationship, each partner has different hopes and dreams, wants and needs, attitudes and experiences. These differences too often result in challenge and disappointment when one or both partners attempt to mold the relationship and their partner to fit what they want, rather than accepting and embracing what is. While we must have a vision and requirements and choose a partner and relationship aligned with what we want, we can't be so rigid that we reject reality.

So, how do we let go of needing perfection without settling for less than what we really want? To do so you must *experience your experience.*

Your Experience

As mentioned in Chapter Three, your "experience" is what happens inside of you. It happens automatically. It's the thoughts that pop into your head, the sensations you have in your body, what you see, hear, feel, touch and taste. It's what you are feeling emotionally.

Your experience just happens. When you go to a movie, you might love the movie and you feel tingly and warm, you have a positive experience of the movie. Or, when you go to a movie and you might hate it and it repulses you, you have a negative experience of the movie.

Your experience is involuntary. It always happens in the now, so you must be present in the now to experience your experience. You can't be in the past, thinking about what was, and you can't be in the future, thinking about what will be.

Relationships only happen in the present.
Connection can only happen in the present.

Relationships only happen in the present. Connection can only happen in the present. To be in touch with what is real for us and to have a fulfilling relationship we must be able to *experience our experience.* In other words, we must see the person for who they are and the relationship for what it is and leave our baggage at the door. We must be present, experiencing what is real, right now, instead of fantasizing about the future or obsessing about the past.

Here are two paradigms to help you experience your experience:

Paradigm #1: Experience/Stories/Actions

Your experience is what's real for you, and you get to decide what it means. Your stories, however, are your interpretation and a direct result of your experience, and lead to actions. Let's get back to our example. If you went to a movie and it repulsed you, then you might create a story such as *"That movie was horrible, maybe even the worst movie ever made."* Your experience leads you to assign it a meaning, about which you might decide to tell everybody you know *"That movie was terrible. Don't see it."* So your stories, which come from your experience, then result in your actions or what you say and do, which directly ties into communication and how you interact with your partner.

Paradigm #2: Facts/Judgments/Feelings

As mentioned in Chapter Three, to effectively *experience your experience*, it is helpful to stay conscious of three of its aspects: facts (what happens to you), judgments (your "stories" about the facts), and your feelings (how you emotionally process the judgments).

> **Facts**—usually a measurable event ("the sky is blue")
> **Judgments**—the meaning we make of the event ("the blue sky is pretty")
> **Feelings**—our emotions and sensations (warm, cold, happy, sad, etc)

---

*We make judgments about something
and try to turn it into a fact.*

Often, what we human beings do, especially when we're upset or excited, is make judgments about something and try to turn it into a fact.

"You make me so angry." "You're a jerk." "I love you." "War is hell." "Ice cream is good." These are all judgments you might feel so strongly about that you believe them to be true. While they might be your personal truth at the time, they are not facts, no matter how strongly you believe them to be true.

It all starts with an event or stimulus. Something happens that gives us a certain experience. Then, we react to our experience by attaching meaning to it and forming judgments. Then, our judgments stimulate our emotions—mad, sad, glad, fear, shame. And this all happens in the blink of an eye. We can then react, consciously or unconsciously.

If we react unconsciously we will act out our feelings and judgments, whatever they are. If we react consciously we will separate the facts from our feelings and judgments and then decide what meanings to make and actions to take. This begins by reviewing the facts in your head and making sure you're not mixing in judgments.

Four Steps for Experiencing Your Experience

Step One: Review the facts
"OK, the sky is blue, we're walking in the park together, the temperature is about 76 degrees, I just said 'It's a beautiful day' and my partner said 'No, it sucks.'"

Step Two: Review your judgments
"Hmm, I believe it's a gorgeous day, walking here is wonderful, and I judge that my partner isn't getting it at all."

Step Three: Identify your feelings
"I'm glad it's such a beautiful day, sad that my partner is troubled and not enjoying it, frustrated and angry at their negativity."

Step Four: Make a conscious choice
Once you've separated the facts from your judgments and feelings you are in a much better position to decide what to think, feel, and how to react. Notice in the above example that the judgments and feelings are mixed, which is common. If you are conscious, you can choose amongst the mix of judgments and feelings that you will embrace and act upon, and which you will discard or leave alone.

In the above example you might decide to focus upon your sadness that your partner is having a bad day and choose a compassionate response, and to discard your judgment that they aren't "getting it."

Experiencing your experience is helpful in getting you into the realm of radical relationships and builds upon The Communication

Map. Additionally, you may want to employ another strategy of Radical Communication that we call The Relationship Journal, covered in the next chapter.

Radical Action:

Next time your partner is upset about something (that may or may not involve you), if they're willing, support them to use the above Four Steps for Experiencing Your Experience to gain clarity and perspective and make a conscious choice about what they're upset about. And next time you're upset about something, talk it out with your partner using these four steps and test if this is a good strategy for handling future frustration and upset.

Chapter Five: Radical Communication
Part 3 - The Relationship Journal

A long time ago David entered a relationship with a woman. He fell in love. He didn't want to ... in fact, she pursued him. He wanted nothing to do with her at first because he just felt they didn't have that much in common; however, she wore him down and won him over.

David and his partner were different people with different priorities, which made things difficult. There was a continuing experience in which they would talk about their relationship, talk about the future, and make agreements. Then she would change her mind later and break the agreements. It drove him crazy!

Still, he had fallen in love with her. He wanted to make the relationship work. Being a guy and being pragmatic and linear, he wanted to pin her down. He felt maybe it would help her keep agreements if they put it in writing. He was trying really hard in the relationship, and all the while he was learning a lot about femininity. She was a very feminine person and a different personality. Now, it seems so obvious: *Of course women change their mind! Expect it.* But back then David didn't have as much understanding of the different personality types and what it was like to be truly feminine.

The conversations they started having about marriage were a red flag for David. He thought, *Shoot, I don't want to live like this for the rest of my life.* So he invited his partner to go on a relationship retreat. While this certainly ties into *Radical Intimacy* and *Radical Romance*, which we will discuss in separate chapters, there was also a *Radical Communication* component. There was an added exercise, a *radical* exercise. David brought along two blank spiral notebooks, and he and his partner tackled *The Relationship Journal.*

The Process

The Relationship Journal started as a way to improve a rocky relationship and developed into a tool that can also be used to help get you and your partner beyond happily ever after to a Radical Marriage.

Start by agreeing on a setting to spend some uninterrupted time together, full of intention to connect and further your relationship. You and your partner will identify what you need, any potential issues and how to address them, and consciously and effectively co-create your relationship and lives together.

After you have set your appointment, you will need two blank notebooks, or whatever you would prefer to write in. You have your journal and your partner has their journal. You will want to have recurring appointments, at least once a week, maybe even more if you're in a phase where you're working more intensely on your relationship. Schedule at least half an hour, preferably more, to work on your Relationship Journal together. For example: "Every Sunday after lunch we're going to take an hour and write in our Relationship Journal and then go through the process of going beyond happily ever after."

It works well if the process is part of your routine.

As you might know, it works well if the process is part of your routine: it's scheduled, each partner knows what to expect and it happens on a regular basis. And when the time comes to work on your Relationship Journal together, don't wait for your partner to remember it or initiate it. Take 100% personal responsibility for the process and for your contribution to the relationship. Although it might drive you crazy if the time came to do your Relationship Journal and your partner was busy doing something else, it never helps to get resentful or mad. It works much better for you to be present and take initiative because it's important to you. Don't wait for your partner to remember or initiate.

In preparation for each session, create an intimate space for the process. Turn off the radio and the television. Make sure that you have privacy. Turn your telephone ringers off. Put your cell phone on vibrate. Light a candle. Put on some soft music. Make some tea. Do whatever contributes to a relaxed, distraction-free intimate atmosphere for you and your partner.

Step One: What do you appreciate about your partner today?

Step One:
What do you appreciate about your partner today?

Start the process by writing in your own Relationship Journal while your partner writes in his or her journal. This process can be anything you want it to be, but here's a suggestion for an entry: *What do you appreciate about your partner today?*

Don't worry about duplication, saying things that you've said before; just answer the question in real time. *What are you in touch with, right now, in this present moment, that you appreciate about your partner?* Be sure to think *who they are* as well as what they *do*.

Step Two: What issues are you aware of in your relationship today?

Step Two:
What issues are you aware of in your relationship today?

Then, after you've done that, answer another question: What issues are you aware of in your relationship today?

In this moment you are contemplating your relationship, looking at your partner. What are you aware of that's getting in the way of intimacy, trust, and connection? What issues are you aware of that exist in your relationship today?

Again, don't worry about duplication. Don't worry about identifying something that you've already talked about or done in the past. If it's present for you, write it down. If it's an ongoing, unsolvable problem that you're still aware of, then it's important. Write it down. What issues are you aware of in your relationship today?

Step Three: What needs and desires can you identify that you are experiencing in your relationship today?

Step Three:
What needs and desires can you identify that you are experiencing in your relationship today?

The third aspect of the entry is, *What needs and desires can you identify that you are experiencing in your relationship today?* While needs often relate to a deficit of some kind, a desire is more related to a *want*. What do you need or want from your partner? What do you need in your relationship right now to have the experience that you really want to have? What do you need to experience the love, trust, and connection that you really want? What do you need to experience the intimacy that you really want? What needs and desires can you identify? Is there anything else that occurs to you?

The second and third categories actually go hand in hand. Each of the responses in the second entry, "What issues are you aware of in your relationship today?" can be turned around into a positive in terms of what it is you need. As we mentioned in Chapter Three, an issue is really an unmet need. Start looking at your issues in a new and creative way, *Okay, what does this say about what I need in this relationship?* So, again, *What needs can you identify that you are experiencing in your relationship today?*

Step Four: Optional Items

What did you do today, or recently,
to improve your relationship?

There are a couple of optional items for an entry in your Relationship Journal. The first is, *What did you do today, or recently, to improve your relationship?* There are several reasons for this. For starters, when something's important to us and we do something to accomplish our goal in it, we want to pat ourselves on the back. We want to acknowledge ourselves for it.

Often, in our daily routine we lose track of our accomplishments. We don't give ourselves enough credit. We forget that we did this wonderful thing and thought of our partner and went to the store and got their favorite coffee or brought them flowers one day or folded their laundry and did things without asking. Acknowledge yourself for the effort that you put into the relationship—not to make your own life better, not for your children, not for some practical, functional thing like paying the bills, but for your relationship.

This also covers what you want your partner to realize, understand, or acknowledge that you've done for the relationship. This is where you say, "Hey, I did this!" If you hadn't received enough acknowledgment, or it's something your partner isn't even aware of that you've done for the relationship, then this is the time that your partner can learn. "Oh, you did that? Oh, thank you so much. I didn't even realize that." Here you get to celebrate and acknowledge each other for the efforts that you have made and are making, even the things that have gone unseen.

Whatever we pay attention to in life will expand. If you pay attention to doing good things for your relationship, then that expands and your relationship becomes better and you want to do

more good things for your relationship and your partner will too. It's a very cool thing.
Bookmarking

Bookmark thoughts, needs, issues, ideas, etc.,
by writing them in your Relationship Journal
as they occur to you.

If you do the Relationship Journal process regularly, then you can bookmark thoughts, needs, issues, ideas, etc., by writing them in your Relationship Journal as they occur to you. During the week, you might do something or think of something, and then remember, "Oh, yeah, I'm going to write this one down." Then during your next Relationship Journal session you can refer back to your notes and experiences as you make your entry.

Sex

---

*Rank your most recent sexual experience
with your partner from one to ten.*

The next optional item is to rank your most recent sexual experience with your partner from one to ten. One is totally bad ... totally sucked ... didn't do a thing for me, and ten is totally mind-blowing ... wonderful ... fulfilled my wildest desires. Then, identify how it could have been a ten for you. If you rated your last sexual experience a six, then what would have been necessary to make it a ten?

In doing this exercise, you and your partner will quickly learn what you need to know about each other to have better and more fulfilling sex. You will learn more about each other's needs. Sometimes it's hard and awkward to talk about sex when your clothes are off. When your clothes are on and you're talking about your relationship that you want to consciously co-create, is a great time to talk about what you need sexually. In short order, you'll find that your rankings of your sexual experiences will start reaching eight, nine, and ten pretty regularly.

Step Five: Swap and Read Each Other's Journals

Step Five:
Swap and read each other's journals.

After you've each taken about twenty minutes to write in your Relationship Journal, then trade. Swap journals and read each other's entry. Ask clarifying questions in a neutral, non-judgmental, non-defensive manner. Here, you just want more information. You're trying to understand where your partner is coming from. Try not to be reactive or have a problem with what they're saying. You want to co-create your relationship. You want your relationship to go beyond *good*. That's why you're doing this. Nobody is at fault here. Nobody is wrong. It's all about *How can we have a fulfilled relationship together?*

If needed, please use The Communication Map. The Communication Map can add structure for how to address an issue or a problem and create emotional safety. So, make some entries, swap journals, read each other's entries, and ask clarifying questions in a neutral non-judgmental, non-defensive manner. Then, after you've read through what your partner wrote, decide who goes first and start by acknowledging your partner's appreciations. Go ahead and read it out loud and acknowledge what your partner appreciates about you and the relationship.

Step Six: Address Issues, Needs and Desires

Step Six:
Address issues, needs and desires.

As you go through the issues, brainstorm and identify the matching need for each issue. It's a mutual process. If your partner has an issue, you want to understand what their need is and how it can be met. It might not even be necessary that you do anything different, but you can assist your partner in getting their need met. But you won't know unless you learn specifically what the need is.

The important thing is for the need to be met,
not how it's met.

Once you have explored each issue and identified the underlying need, you can negotiate the needs one by one. Talk about how to meet each one of those needs. Be open, be flexible, and find a win-win solution. There are many ways to meet a need, so do your best to remain free and flexible. "No, this is what I want to have happen. I want it to happen this way." That kind of rigidity actually interferes with the relationship. Remember, the important thing is for the need to be met, not how it's met. Find a way to meet the need that will work for both of you.

If you find yourselves stuck, and sometimes you will get stuck, it's good to recognize that there is such a thing as unsolvable problems. Put it on the shelf for now and go on to the next one. Go through the process until you've gone through all the needs that have been identified. For the ones that you're stuck on, or the ones that you're not quite satisfied with the solutions; do some research, get ideas from friends and family and professionals and books and magazines and anywhere else. Have an open-minded attitude and assume that there is a creative solution somewhere. Just because you can't see it right away doesn't mean it doesn't exist.

In essence, in addressing issues, needs and desires, what you're doing is making agreements. You're going to agree upon a solution and somebody will be responsible for implementing the solution. Sometimes it's something that one person is going to be doing differently. Sometimes it's something that both people are going to be doing differently. In your Relationship Journal, record the agreements that you're responsible for implementing. These are the things that *you* will do differently. Your partner does the same thing in their Relationship Journal. They record the agreements that *they* will do differently.

In a relationship we are often aware of what we want our partner to do differently. That's easy. What's not so easy, and what the Relationship Journal process might highlight and communicate, are the things that we can do differently to have our own needs met. It's the idea of ownership. It's the idea that what we do and say and how we show up in the relationship either helps us or prevents our needs from being met.

Ownership

As we touched upon earlier, you have thoughts and feelings and wants and needs and interpretations and meanings and stories that you create in your own head, and we need to be 100% responsible for our own experience. It's coming from inside us.

---

*It's not our partner's fault that we feel a certain way
or think a certain thing.*

It's not our partner's fault that we feel a certain way or think a certain thing. They might be the trigger, they might be the stimulus, but so might be the wall, or the tree, or the news report. It's not the outside world's fault that we have the internal experience that we're having. The Relationship Journal process really helps in this regard. *Okay, what do I want my partner to do? Let's talk about it. But also, what can I do differently to get my own need met?*

When you make agreements or plans about how to make the relationship better and how to meet your needs or your partner's needs, you must write down the agreements that you are responsible for implementing. If there's a start date or there's some sort of measurability to it, then write that down as well. *Bring home flowers at least three times a week after work* is an example of a measurable outcome.

You might know this already, but for solutions or goals to be effective, they need to be positive, measurable, and specific— PMS. Positive is, *What is going to happen as opposed to not happen?* Measurable is, *How often we do this or how we quantify it.* Specific is, *When, Where, What, How, Who?* Again, record the agreements that you are responsible for in your Relationship Journal. Your partner will do the same.

Now, there are a couple of assumptions to make here. As we discussed before, *all* needs are valid. There is no arguing about it. Still, sometimes that can be a challenge. If a need is something we don't agree with, or if it violates our values or our morals, or if we don't like it, then we just want it to go away. The reality is, if it's a need that our partner experiences, it's valid. It's not going to go away on its own, though a solution may appear seemingly out of nowhere or due to a change in circumstance. In the meantime, if a need is unmet, it creates an issue, every time.

No need can be sacrificed in a successful relationship.

No need can be sacrificed in a successful relationship. We must assume that a solution exists. We must assume that there's a way to meet this need that works for both of us. But that doesn't make it an easy riddle to solve. Sometimes it's challenging to hold on to this belief or assumption. "I need to live on the West Coast by my family, and you need to live on the East Coast by your family, and living in the middle of the country in Nebraska is not going to work for either of us. How can we meet our needs? What's the win-win here?"

Stay optimistic. Be open-minded, flexible, and creative. If you're brainstorming and what you know and what you can think of doesn't work, then do some more research. Seek assistance. Ask

111

friends and family. Get some professional help. Read through some books. Do what you have to do, but don't give up, ever.

There is no such thing as a unique relationship challenge.

There is no such thing as a unique relationship challenge. Millions of other people in the world have experienced the exact same challenge in their life or relationship. How did they solve it? Hold on to that. Sure, nobody has had your exact relationship before; however, what happens in a relationship is the human condition. Many others have encountered the same thing. You may have to put in some time and effort to find it, but know that there is a solution out there somewhere.

In some situations, it's possible that solutions aren't even going to be needed. Sometimes problems solve themselves. Sometimes they just go away over time because nothing is static. Nothing ever stays the same. Over time, what once seemed so urgent and important might not be so important anymore. Eventually you might not even have that need anymore.

Regardless, record all your agreements and the solutions in the Relationship Journal, and, of course, keep all your agreements. That's your goal. But nobody's perfect, and it's not always going to work out as planned. If you find yourself in an argument and it is becoming too stressful, then stop. If you're experiencing frustration and stress and you're starting to argue, stop. It is much more productive to call time out, take a break, and pick it up at another time. You can make an agreement as to when. *"How about we reconvene after dinner, tomorrow?"* or *"Let's put this on the shelf for next week."*

---

*It's much better to keep the process productive
and positive for both of you than to try
to argue your way through it.*

Making adjustments is just fine. It's much better to keep the process productive and positive for both of you than to try to argue your way through it. If you really can't do it on your own, and some couples can't, then it might be helpful to use a professional facilitator for a while. Go through this process with a relationship professional until you can get through the process productively and handle the disagreements and the differences and reactivity and whatever else comes up.

Step Seven: Closing Ritual

However you choose to go through the Relationship Journal, we recommend a closing ritual. Make it official. Lock it in. Reward your efforts. Make a big deal of it. You've created the intimate space, picked the time and place and day, and written in your own journal. You've answered, *What do you appreciate about your partner today? What issues are you aware of in your relationship today? What needs can you identify that you're experiencing in your relationship today? What did you do today or recently to improve your relationship?* You've ranked your most recent sexual experience with your partner from one to ten and identified how it could have been a ten.

Next you've read each other's entry, asked clarifying questions in a neutral, non-judgmental, non-defensive manner, and started by acknowledging your partner's appreciations. You've taken turns, focusing on one person, then the other. You've looked at the issues and made sure every issue has an identified need that would address that issue. You've negotiated and strategized over the needs one by one on how they are going to be met and made an agreement on who's going to do what.

You've written all of the agreements in your Relationship Journal. Your partner has written all the agreements that they are responsible for in their Relationship Journal. Some agreements are unilateral—they are things that you alone will do. Other agreements are mutual—they are things that both of you will do. You've recorded these agreements, kept the agreements you could, changed the ones you couldn't. You've discussed, "Okay, this is what we're going to do in our relationship between now and next time." Now you're ready to close.

A closing ritual is nice. It can be as simple as a hug and a kiss. It can be as simple as putting the journal down and doing a mutual meditation or praying together or singing. What's important is to co-create a closing ritual that helps you connect and be close and aligned in your consciousness of your relationship and being in each other's life and each other's space together.

Summary of Relationship Journal Steps

Step One: Meet at agreed place and time, open your journal, and write what you appreciate about your partner today.
Step Two: What issues are you aware of in your relationship today?
Step Three: What needs and desires can you identify that you're experiencing in your relationship today?
Step Four: Optional items: What have you done recently for your relationship? Rate your last sexual experience from 0 to 10 and identify what would make it a "10" for you.
Step Five: Swap and read each other's journal
Step Six: Address issues, needs and desires
Step Seven: Closing Ritual

The Relationship Journal is a great tool for a self-guided, romantic relationship retreat which we'll describe in more detail in Chapter Eight: Radical Romance.

So that's the *Relationship Journal*, and it works well with the *Communication Map* and as a way to integrate *Radical Communication* in your life to foster a *Radical Marriage*. They are foundational elements for dealing effectively with conflict. And as you gain entry to the next level of your relationship, like *experiencing your experience,* you may be ready for higher-order strategies. With that, let's take a look at *asserting your boundaries and telling your truth* as additional principles of *Radical Communication.*

Chapter Six: Radical Communication
Part 4 - Living Your Truth

Creating safety for yourself in a relationship centers around truth, assertiveness, and boundaries. These are the first of several strategies for *Radical Intimacy*, the subject of our next chapter, but are also applicable for *Radical Communication*. As a way of diving deeper into this topic, we must first note that while there is some overlap between intimacy and communication, there is a definite distinction between the two.

Intimacy is the experience that you are having
with your partner and communication is what you do.

Intimacy is the experience that you are having with your partner and *communication* is what you do, the means by which you experience your relationship. As a further distinction, there is communication for intimacy, which is a way of connecting and getting closer to your partner, and communication for self-advocacy, which is a way of getting your needs met, which is the purpose of telling your truth, assertiveness, and boundaries, and the focus of this chapter.

Self-Advocacy

We all want our partner to support us and be there for us. But we also know that this is the real world, and in reality, we need to look out for number one. While there is nothing inherently wrong with that, a lot of people feel selfish for even thinking about it. Still, to have a strong relationship you must have a strong sense of self, and to have a strong sense of self, you must be clear about who you are, what you want, and what's true for you. You must take care of yourself and speak up when you are having a hard time. This is what we refer to as self-advocacy, and it generally takes two forms: *reactive assertiveness* and *proactive assertiveness*.

Reactive Assertiveness

Reactive assertiveness is what most of us are familiar with—it's when somebody steps on our toe, we say "ouch!" and kindly ask them to step off.

From the checker at the grocery store who doesn't give us the correct change to the delivery person who doesn't deliver our newspaper in the morning, there are many, benign situations in the world where somebody does or does not do something that infringes on our boundaries. It's up to us to take action to correct it. We need to take care of ourselves and do or say something to assert our boundaries and get our needs met.

---

*Advocating for our needs is a responsibility
we cannot delegate.*

The wish or expectation that others will step up for us tends to not work well. Even if our best interests are in fact considered by others, like the love of our life, we can't expect them to read our mind or automatically do things when and how we want them to be done. Advocating for our needs is a responsibility we cannot delegate. We must step up and assert our own self-identified needs and boundaries.

Boundaries

You are absolutely never going to be satisfied, and life or a relationship is never really going to work for you if you expect other people, even the one that loves you the most, to magically anticipate or figure out your needs and boundaries for you. There are very few absolutes in the world that we would feel confident stating, but this is one of them.

It's rarely a good idea to say always and never, but we can confidently assert that you will never, ever be satisfied ... you will never get your needs met ... you will always be let down ... things will never work for you ... if you expect other people to read your mind, figure out your boundaries, or meet your needs the way you want them to be met without you having to say or do anything.

You need to speak up and assert yourself, which effectively means that you must know the location of your boundaries, those lines in life and relationships between what is okay and what is not okay for you.

Here's an example: Last week the paper delivery person threw our newspaper in the sprinklers. Our paper was wet and we couldn't read it. This crossed a boundary and was not okay for us, so David took action. He requested another paper and we got another paper. Chances are that won't happen again because David spoke up. If he didn't speak up, even though where not to put the newspaper might seem to be common sense, the delivery person might have continued to throw the newspaper in the sprinklers, and over and over again we would have an unreadable paper. As a result, we would be disappointed and frustrated. Even though it may be foreign or difficult at times, there is nothing fundamentally wrong with looking out for yourself and your best interests. In fact, we would argue that it's necessary for fulfillment.

If you are in a park and somebody near you lights up a cigarette and it bothers you, then you have a choice to make. You could say something and risk a conflict, or you could simply step away and relocate yourself. Either way, in this case, if you don't take care of yourself and assert your boundaries, then you will angrily sit there breathing in second-hand smoke and you will feel bad about yourself for not doing anything about it.

Not asserting our needs and boundaries increases our stress and affects our physical and emotional health. What's more, if you are unable to take care of yourself, and at the minimum summon the ability to exercise reactive assertiveness, you will not live the life that you want and you certainly won't have the relationship that you want. But there's always more you can do, and it starts with taking action ahead of time.

Proactive Assertiveness

If you want to ensure things go smoothly in your life, though it's a strategy that is a little less common, you can take care of yourself in advance of an event. This is called *proactive assertiveness.*

It's far more effective to be proactively assertive and speak up in advance for something that you want or need than to address it after it's happened.

For example, let's say you don't like being seated close to the kitchen when you go out to eat, because you find it too noisy to talk. When you arrive at the restaurant you could say, "We prefer a quiet table please." If you don't speak up for your table preference ahead of time you risk being seated at a table that prevents you from talking, which forces you to be reactively assertive to get your needs met. It's far more effective to be proactively assertive and speak up in advance for something that you want or need than to address it after it's happened.

Here's another way to think about it: *Reactive assertiveness* would be taking care of your car when there's a problem and something breaks down. *Proactive assertiveness* would be preventative maintenance and addressing things ahead of time, because you know if you don't there will be problems down the road. With a bit of forethought things tend to operate more smoothly and reliably and your life is more pleasant all around.

It may come as a surprise, but people are generally willing to modify their behavior upon request in relationships if there is something that you need. It's even better if they don't have to step in doo-doo for that to happen. Your partner will generally be more receptive when you are not in a position of correcting them or having to change something that's already taken place. It's much easier and more efficient if things go well the first time, as opposed to picking up the pieces after someone failed to meet your needs or infringed upon your boundaries.

Telling Your Truth

If you are ever to reach the level of *Radical Communication*, it is crucial that you tell your truth, which comes in three forms. There is the *conscious truth*, which is the truth that you are aware of; there is the *semiconscious truth*, which is the truth that is just below the surface; and then there is the *unconscious truth*, which is the truth that gets uncovered only when you are looking for it or through learning more about yourself.

---

*Nothing ever occurs just once
and nothing is ever random.*

As for speaking our mind, it should really be a no-brainer that we would at least tell our conscious truth, and that the way to a good relationship and to take care of ourselves is to simply say what we are thinking. But we are human, and as such, we are subject to the reality that behavior follows patterns. In other words, nothing ever occurs just once and nothing is ever random.

Behavior Follows Patterns

Sometimes we avoid being assertive and hope the problem will go away or won't happen again. But if we accept that behavior follows patterns and nothing ever occurs just once, then we can anticipate our own needs and boundaries. *That didn't work for me in the past, so maybe I should try something different.* Proactive assertiveness and reactive assertiveness can work together and paying attention can help us learn more about our truth. Realizing that what we experience is going to come up again enables us to address what we are going to do about it next time, and better yet, how we can prevent it from happening in the first place.

Asserting ourselves, even if it's not conflict,
often feels like conflict.

Still, even if we recognize the benefits of being proactive, it's natural to avoid conflict. Asserting ourselves, even if it's not conflict, often feels like conflict. It seems risky to tell our truth because we know people get defensive, which can lead to arguments. That's where our communication skills come in handy and we make requests instead of relying on the alternatives like complaining, criticizing, and threatening. Requesting is respectful, and if you phrase things in a non-judgmental way, you can tell your truth without making anybody wrong, which, for the most part, is pretty well received.

If, on the other hand, your words come out with a judgmental tone or emotional energy behind them, as if you are upset, angry, or resentful, then your truth could stimulate conflict and defensiveness. Thinking back to the Communication Map, this is where we encounter known roadblocks such as judgment, interpretation, defensiveness, and reactive emotion. In Radical Communication, our job is to tell our truth and assert our boundaries effectively. To do that, we must make requests calmly and respectfully. It's far easier to do that when we are being proactively assertive rather than reactively assertive.

Risk

Although telling our truth can be scary because we fear judgment and conflict, the real risk is in choosing to keep our feelings to ourselves. That increases our chances of not having our needs met, experiencing frustration or resentment, and not having the relationship work for us. So, if we tell our truth, make a request, and assert our boundaries, yes, we risk conflict and defensiveness. But we are also more likely to get our needs met, create closeness, and have our relationships work effectively.

We always have this choice point, and because behavior follows patterns, the choice that you make tends to be repetitive. If you choose to censor yourself to avoid conflict, that tends to occur again and again. You don't ever do it just once. You don't ever do it randomly. That becomes your pattern. If you consistently take the risk to tell your truth and make the request to have your needs met as effectively as you can and assert your boundaries, then that becomes your pattern, which is what *Radical Communication* is all about, and one of the pillars of *Radical Marriage*.

It's Not About You

Support your partner in feeling what they are feeling and you realize it's not about you.

As we mentioned earlier, in a Radical Marriage we create safety for each other. This allows us to be vulnerable and to experience frustration, which is not a negative thing. Yes, it's okay to be annoyed and upset. It's okay to be irrational. "I know I shouldn't be so upset about this, but I am." When you are partners and you allow each other to be who you are and feel what you are feeling and experience your experience, then that's okay. You don't take it personally. You support your partner in feeling what they are feeling and you realize it's not about you.

One of David's mentors once taught him a valuable lesson about relationships: If there is a negative emotion coming up for someone, typically 90% of that emotion is related to the past. In other words, when there is a sense of frustration swirling around, only 10% of it is related to the current situation. Looking through that lens, it is evident that if your partner is upset about something, 90% of that is probably not about you; it's probably a past experience that has been triggered. When you see the situation for what it really is you won't take it so personally.

Remember, positive intention can alleviate a lot of the perceived conflict, and you can't control how people will receive a question from you, nor should you want to. In fact, the attempt to control is a problem, because that's where we get into censoring ourselves. Rather than censoring ourselves, trying to make sure that our partner is okay, we should put effort into communicating our truth as cleanly and clearly as possible, knowing that if people take it wrong it's on them; it's not because we did anything wrong. It's always okay to tell our truth as long as we own it, and it's always okay to make a request as long as we let go of attachment to it.

Reality Check – It Might Be About You

If someone has an issue with you or a judgment about you, whether it's your partner or anyone else, "it's not about you" doesn't mean you are rigidly closed and defensive. While we need to have boundaries and be assertive about them, we also need to remember that our relationships are our mirrors and we have to assume that something about ourselves is getting reflected back. We must take an honest look in the mirror, do a reality check, and evaluate what part of their issue or judgment is valid for us. As mentioned in the "Rules of the Road" of the Communication Map, we assume all issues are valid so we can't summarily dismiss their issue or judgment simply because we disagree with it, but we can consciously decide what part of their truth is true for us and what to do about it

Owning Your Truth

*Owning your truth means that you realize
that it's your truth; it's not the truth.*

Owning your truth means that you realize that it's *your* truth; it's not *the* truth. In *Radical Communication* you realize that it's okay for people to disagree or think or believe differently. It means you will absolutely and cleanly stand up for *your* truth, but you will not present it as fact.

In telling your truth, it may be helpful to attach some sort of language to it like, "this is about me ..." or "In my opinion ..." or "It seems to me ... " or "What's real for me is ..." But these are merely tactics, tools that you can use to help you assert yourself. However you choose to do it, you must be authentic when telling your truth. So, rather than using sentence stems or certain fallback words, we would prefer that you focus on the overall strategy of telling your truth, taking responsibility, staying real, and finding a way that works best for you.

It's worth noting that when we give examples, they are just that—examples. We don't believe that our way is the best and only way to do things. We assume there are many better ways to do it than our way. We are merely presenting the best way we know for right now.

Anytime you state your reality, you must be careful not to infer that your partner must believe it, too. You don't want to get caught up in trying to couch your truth as fact. A fact is observable and measurable, so if I am communicating something that is my truth, and it's not a fact, I need to be clean about it and own it by saying so. Then I can make a request about it. "What I need is ..." or "What I want is ..." or "What I require is ..."

Owning your truth takes the concepts of requirements, needs, and wants, and puts them in communication in a clean way. Owning your truth means you are specific. "What I *want* is this ..." Choosing the word *want* infers a willingness to be flexible and to let go of the request.

If you say, "What I *need* is this ..." then it's a sign that this is very important to you, it's going to be a problem for you if it's not met, and you must connect with your partner about how to make that happen. But you must also acknowledge that there are lots of ways it could be met, and you would like to work with your partner to get it met.

Saying, "I require this ..." is strong language that this is non-negotiable. This has to happen for you or else there are going to be dire consequences for the relationship. The important thing is to make it clear where you are coming from.

It's Always Okay to Tell Your Truth

It's always okay to tell your truth as long as you own it.

We, the authors, believe it's always okay to tell your truth as long as you own it and as long as you are being clean about it. It's always okay to tell your truth as long as you understand and indicate that this is *your* truth, it's not *the* truth, and you are not imposing it on anybody else and you allow them to have a different truth. You must be clear in your attitude and your language that this is about you, not your partner. "I'm not trying to control how you see or think about things or what you do; I'm just sharing with you what's true for me."

Incorporating it's-about-me language into your communication is a much more effective and powerful way of telling your truth, asserting your boundaries, and expressing your needs, and it's a great way to avoid unnecessary conflict. But with some people, no matter what, they will have a problem with what you say if it doesn't mirror them. The idea of mirroring is interesting in that relationships tend to be our mirrors—the way our partner responds to us is a direct reflection of what we put out.

Again, we can do our best to be clean and own something and yet people will sometimes have a problem with it. We can't be afraid of that, though, because if we hold back to avoid conflict it will become a pattern and we will constantly censor ourselves and only asserting ourselves if we anticipate that it would be okay with somebody else.

We cannot treat relationships as a popularity contest. That's not going to create a happy, fulfilling life and relationship. Perhaps for some people, being popular and well-liked is enough to attain fulfillment because they don't want anything more than that, even if it means living a lie, or at best, an incomplete truth. For most of us, however, we need to be who we are and we need to live and express our truth, even if there's risk that some people will take our truth the wrong way or react negatively to it.

So, it's always okay to tell your truth as long as you do it cleanly and you own it and allow others to have a different truth. And it's always okay to make a request as long as you aren't too attached to the outcome, meaning you are not set on exactly how it happens, or on it even happening at all.

Letting Go of Attachment

Let's get back to our smoking example. If you are in a situation where somebody near you lights up a cigarette and it bothers you, you could make a request. "Excuse me, this is a no-smoking area and your smoking does bother me, could you smoke someplace else?" Now, there is a good chance that the person will look at you, sneer, scoff, and say, in effect, "Mind your own business."

As long as you are willing to let go of your request, and take care of yourself in other ways, say by removing yourself, rather than needing to control other people's behavior, you should be okay. Yes, it's still risky to speak up, but again, the consequence of not giving yourself permission to make a request, in the most clean way, where you take ownership of it, is that you assure yourself that you will not live your truth.

Remember, your communication does not have to be confrontational—you are not judging and you are not blaming, you are simply taking care of yourself in a clean way, in which you assert that this is your need, so you are making a request about it.

You are both owning your truth and leaving room for your request not to be fulfilled. You are not attached to the outcome; you are attached to your truth.

---

*Most conflict happens because people are
attached to an outcome.*

Most conflict happens because people are attached to an outcome. They are attached to having the other person agree with them and see things their way. Attachment really is the bane of our existence and the bane of relationships. If you get attached to it being a sunny day, well, what if it's not sunny that day? Does that guarantee you're going to have a bad day? If you just let the weather be what it is, and roll with it, you will have a much happier life.

There aren't many ways the role of attachment works well for us. It's certainly a good thing to have a goal, to be committed to that goal, and to have the self-discipline to go for it. But it's also a good thing to not be too attached to exactly what happens or how it happens. Maybe you will never achieve that goal or maybe you will achieve only part of the goal. Does it mean your life is over or you will not be happy or okay if you come up short? At some point you have to let go and allow things to be what they are.

You can see the role of attachment and the need to let go of attachment throughout life and throughout Radical Marriage. It's all over the place. It comes into play in *Radical Intimacy* and *Radical Commitment*, and it comes into play in *Radical Communication.* If you are attached to somebody else agreeing with you, or doing what you want them to do, or controlling them with your words, then your communication is not going to be very effective. In fact, it's likely to result in conflict. But if you are not attached to things always going your way, and you are just telling your truth, making a request, and being clean about it and owning it, then your communication will be much more effective and promote a good relationship.

In life and in love we must deal with reality. You will get cut off on the highway. It will rain. People will light up a cigarette where they are not supposed to. You and your partner will have disagreements. You can't stumble through life always hoping for things to be different, wishing things had happened the way you wanted them to happen or that people always followed the rules. You must be willing to accept that *life is what it is,* and when you don't get your needs met you need to speak up or do something about it. That is a necessary thing, that's an okay thing, and that's just part of life. Assertiveness shouldn't be this thing that you resent having to do or that you should avoid because it only creates problems.

We are not perfect and we need to accept that. We must allow ourselves to be who we are and love ourselves as we are, and we must remember that our partner is not perfect either. We must love them for who they are. We can't keep up a persona for very long, nor can they, so why even bother?
Relationships Keep Us Honest

It's hard to hide forever in a relationship. You can put on a happy face, you can play act like you've got it all together and that you are calm, cool, and collected, but if that is an act, if you are playing a role, then you are not going to be able to keep it up for very long. **Relationships keep us honest**—that's what they do. They reveal who we really are. In a relationship, it's hard to cover up our truth, our reality, our warts, our faults, and our vices. Nor should we want to. Think of the pain and deception that comes from hiding our truth all the time. Besides, everything will come out eventually, so we might as well accept it and allow it to come out.

We must own who we are, which means standing up for it and telling the truth about it.

It's a package deal.
We must accept the quirks along with everything else.

In a Radical Marriage, full disclosure is not only accepted and supported, it's expected. In relationships that don't work very well or even in *good* marriages, the truth is often judged. And it's rejected. "Well, I like this part of you and this part of you, but I don't like that part of you and that part of you." That's not realistic. That's not the way relationships work. It's a package deal. We must accept the quirks along with everything else.

Here's the cool part: When you have safety and are in an environment where you are truly accepted for who you are, and you allow each other to experience your experience without judgment, then you will relish *Radical Communication* in your relationship. You will be able to accept your partner's truth and experience and tell your truth, always.

There's Always Something New

The great adventure in a relationship is that there is always something new. There is always something new to learn about yourself and there is always something new to learn about your partner. What's more, we change and evolve over time. So, it's not just discovering things that were there that we never noticed before; it's discovering things that only recently developed. Just when we think we know our partner 100% they surprise us with some aspect of them that we never knew existed, that we are still discovering and that we haven't experienced before—and it often comes out in reaction to something.

Let's say you and your partner are watching a movie and your partner starts crying during a particular scene, and they don't even know why. Eventually they will get in touch with their truth and

129

what caused that scene to touch them so deeply. In so doing, they learn more about themselves and you learn more about them.

Situations like these come up all the time in everyday life and in relationships. There is always something you will react to that will reveal more of who you are and who your partner is. And as more truth gets revealed, your job as partners is to share it with each other. Even if you choose not to share it, your partner will sometimes pick up on it anyway—they can often see it right in front of them. It's not always something that you talk about, but it is something that you ideally would embrace and share with each other rather than try to keep it to yourselves.

---

*When you keep things to yourself
you live inside a rigid box.*

When you keep things to yourself you live inside a rigid box. "Here's who I am. Here's how I think about myself. Here's who you are. Here's how I think of you—and that can't change." No, when we try to box ourselves in to fit a strict idea of who we are and who we want to be, or a strict idea of who we want our partner to be, it doesn't work and it creates barriers or false boundaries.

Unearthing More about Yourself and Your Partner

A Radical Marriage is all about the never-ending adventure of discovering more about who you are, which tends to come out anyway. As we've stated, it's impossible to hide in a relationship, and there are things that were always there that you are just now discovering for the first time, and there are things that arise as you change, grow, and evolve over time. In either case, the ongoing adventure of learning more about yourself and your partner is one of the true benefits and joys of marriage.

---

*You can be with somebody for a long time
and continue to discover new things about them.*

It's a fascinating idea that you can be with somebody for a long time and continue to discover new things about them. It's like archaeology—discovering this *find* that was dormant for years. "Where'd that come from? That's a surprise!"

Discovery is part of the adventure of relationships, and in a Radical Marriage you embrace it, encourage it, and accept it when it happens. You even seek it, going after it rather than waiting for it to come to you.

The Relationship Journal is a great tool for seeking discovery. As we broaden our communication and deepen our intimacy, we will naturally learn more about our partner and the deeper we will go. After all, we are able to go much deeper together than we can individually.

It Takes Continuous Effort

It's your responsibility to tell your truth, to identify and assert your boundaries. You are responsible to communicate positively and to make requests instead of complaints. You must be proactively assertive as best you can and reactively assertive when the situation calls for it.

Telling your truth is one of those things
that you can never get too good at.

Telling your truth is one of those things that you can never get too good at. You never arrive. There is never a destination. You are never the expert. You always need to put effort into it. The more work you put into it the better you'll get, and the better your life and relationship will be. But it does take continuous effort. It never feels smooth. It always feels like you are expending energy and thought to improve.

In any communication exchange we can identify a way that it could have been more effective. We are human beings and we are imperfect. We get better with practice. We get better with intention. *Radical Communication* is embracing the idea that you need to put effort into relating your truth. You must never be complacent. You must learn and hone your skills, and your partner is always around to give you practice. That's a good thing, because no matter how good you become in the realm of communication, it can always be better.

Relationships are about communication. It's what makes them work or not. The *Communication Map* addresses conflict and the *Relationship Journal* is wonderful for co-creating your relationship, but in the context of communication, these tools tend to be more basic, foundational stuff. *Experiencing your experience, asserting your boundaries and needs,* and *telling your truth* comprise higher-order communication skills and functioning. Strive for that, and you and your partner will find yourselves squarely on the path to *Radical Communication and a Radical Marriage.*

Radical Action:

Strive to catch yourself holding back your truth to avoid conflict and make a conscious choice rather than following an unconscious habit or pattern. While it's true you might need to "pick your battles" in the world, for a Radical Marriage you must risk conflict and tell your truth, always. And keep an eye on your partner; check in with them if they appear to be holding something back and reassure them it's safe to tell you their truth.

Chapter Seven: Radical Intimacy

When we invite someone to be intimate with us, we are opening up our world. That's what intimacy means: "Into me I see." In a couple relationship we want to be respected and loved for who we really are, and we can't do that if we're not telling each other the truth. If intimacy is opening ourselves up, then *Radical Intimacy* is granting access on a whole new level.

The dictionary generally defines *intimacy* as a close, familiar and usually affectionate or loving personal relationship with another person. For couples, we define intimacy as sharing your private thoughts, feelings, wants and needs in a close emotional and physical relationship.

These are things that you usually wouldn't share with anyone else.

We use the word *private* because these are things that you usually wouldn't share with anyone else. It means *this* relationship is special and clearly different from other relationships, like your roommate, colleagues, friends, or family members.

Radical Intimacy goes even further than "regular" intimacy. Besides sharing your private thoughts, feelings, wants, and needs, *Radical Intimacy* includes fears and secrets and fantasies and desires—everything inside you, without holding anything back. In addition to *emotional* and *physical intimacy*, we also include *spiritual intimacy*.

Does that sound scary?

It is.

Radical Intimacy requires a tremendous amount of trust, risk-taking, emotional maturity, self-confidence, and self-knowledge, but it's incremental. It's not like jumping into the deep end of the pool all at once; it's more like dipping your toe in, following it up with your foot to further test the waters. First you share one little thing. Then another. Next you discover something underneath that, and something else underneath that. Before you know it you're sharing the biggest, most embarrassing fantasy or desire that you've never told anybody—one that you never wanted to even admit to yourself.

How high, far, and deep do you want to go?

The amount of information about yourself that you are willing to share with your partner is in direct correlation to your desired level of intimacy. Given this truth, you must answer several questions: What kind of relationship do you want with your partner? Do you want to live like roommates? Or do you want more? How high, far, and deep do you want to go? Do you want a "normal" relationship? Or do you want an extraordinary relationship?

If you want a great relationship, one that goes beyond happily ever after, a high-level of intimacy is required. If you want a *radical* relationship, your level of intimacy must reach into the *radical*. That's what this chapter is all about—exploring ways to dramatically increase intimacy in your relationship. Here are ten strategies for doing so.

Ten Strategies for Creating Radical Intimacy in Your Marriage

Radical Intimacy Strategy #1: Create Safety for Yourself

We all need boundaries in life and in love. As discussed in Chapter Six, a boundary is that line between what's okay and what's not okay for you as it relates to your partner. It's up to you to identify, communicate, and protect your boundaries. This is how to create safety for yourself, and to do so, you need to be assertive.

Assertiveness is speaking up when your needs are challenged. It's standing up for yourself and articulating your thoughts, and maybe even anticipating when your needs are being encroached upon. As described in Chapter Six, you don't always have to be reactive, you can be proactive. You must empower yourself and take responsibility for your comfort and safety. It's not up to anybody else in the world to do so. It starts with you, and it requires a strong ego.

If you have a fragile ego, or if you are easily offended or hurt, then you're going to be defensive and feel like you're being attacked. If you have a strong ego, then you won't get bogged down in trivial matters. For instance, if you were driving down the street and somebody yelled, "You jerk!" you would evaluate what he said as honestly as possible (did you cut him off by mistake?) and if it doesn't ring true you would determine that it's not about you. You did a reality check and you're not being a jerk; you're just driving down the street minding your own business and it's possible he was yelling at someone else.

That's what it's like when you have a strong ego. Somebody can say something about you, but if you examine what they're saying as honestly as possible (remember, relationships are our mirrors so they might be reflecting what you're putting out) and if it doesn't ring true for you, you don't take it in. You're not defensive about it. "Well, okay, you can say that, but I did my reality check and don't agree with it. I'm just minding my own business and doing my thing." To allow yourself to be truly intimate with your partner, you must *create safety for yourself*. For more on this topic, refer back to Chapter Six.

Radical Action:

Next time you catch yourself tolerating something that bugs you, make a conscious effort to speak up and make a request. Watch how often you hold back from asserting the truth about your needs and work on changing that pattern.

Radical Intimacy Strategy #2: Create Safety for Your Partner

If you are ever going to reach radical levels of intimacy, you must also create safety for your partner. Creating safety for your partner means that you love and accept your partner as they are and you reserve judgment. You take responsibility for your reactions. You support your partner and accept them for who they are, including their thoughts, feelings, wants, and needs. If you can assume there is no wrong—no wrong thought, no wrong feeling, no wrong want, or no wrong need—then every single thought, feeling, want, or need that they have is okay. You might not agree with it. It might not be yours. But you allow them to have it and you support them to have it.

Creating safety for your partner requires unconditional acceptance and non-judgment. If your partner says, "Gee, I've been thinking about that sexy neighbor-lady down the street," you must allow your partner to have that thought, and not make a big deal about it. You must not be defensive about it or make them wrong for having it.

If you want your partner to share their inner world with you
they need to know it's emotionally safe to do so.

137

Generally, a lot of our thoughts, feelings, wants and needs are involuntary. They just happen. We don't choose to have a particular thought. If your partner is thinking about the sexy person down the street, it's not because they voluntarily decide to do it: "You know what? I'm going to choose to think about that person right now!" Generally, thoughts just come up. It's part of the human experience. Your partner is going to have thoughts anyway, would you rather they keep to themselves or would you want them shared with you? If you want your partner to share their inner world with you they need to know it's emotionally safe to do so.

The good news about creating safety for your partner is that if you are practicing *Radical Commitment* (Chapter Two), chances are you're already doing this. You are already embracing them fully for who they are, 100%. You are prioritizing their happiness. You know that it is okay for your partner to be who they are, and you are not going anywhere. That is part of creating safety for your partner.

By the way, we fully acknowledge that this is not necessarily easy. This is where putting effort and consciousness into your relationship is important. You may even want to get the support of a relationship coach. Regardless of how you get there, you must realize that Radical Intimacy requires you to love your partner for who they are. You must not make them wrong for having any particular thought, feeling, want, or need. That's how you *create safety for your partner.*

Radical Action:

Check in with your partner about how emotionally safe and accepted they feel with you. Ask that they let you know when they perceive that you're being judgmental of them so you can adjust your attitude and work on accepting your differences.

Radical Intimacy Strategy #3: Continually Take Risks

If it's scary, you're doing it right.

The wonderful thing about a long-term relationship is that you can build trust and shared experiences over time. You can get to know each other well and there is always more to explore. There is always more to share, there is always more to learn about your partner, and it's not going to happen if you refuse to take risks.

Taking a risk means that you're going to say something or put yourself out there in a way that you haven't done before. That's how you push the envelope. That is how you grow. That is how a relationship evolves and becomes truly adventurous.

In a relationship, being adventurous doesn't mean jumping out of a plane with a parachute. Being adventurous in a relationship means going deeper than you've gone before, and revealing things that are more private to you, things that in the past you haven't felt comfortable sharing. But the longer you get to know somebody and have a relationship with them, the more you are able to trust them. Gradually, you can reveal yourself more fully and develop a heightened level of intimacy.

Safety is important, but if you remain focused on it exclusively, it will help you feel okay, but it won't make your life exciting and help you evolve and get to the next level. The way to get to the next level and go beyond happily ever after is to continually take risks.

If you have a boring relationship
it means you're not being intimate enough.

Intimacy is exciting. If you ever wonder how to make your relationship new and fresh— think intimacy. If you have a boring relationship it means you're not being intimate enough, and part of intimacy is risk, a great example of which is sharing a fantasy or desire. It doesn't even have to be one that you feel good about. In fact, it can be one that you would rather not have.

Sharing a desire doesn't mean you're going to do it; it means that you are enjoying a Radical Marriage by practicing Radical

Intimacy. Yes, if you share a fantasy with your partner it's going to feel like a tremendous risk. *My partner's going to judge me, my partner's going to reject me, my partner's going to think less of me, this might hurt my partner's feelings.* The work in a Radical Marriage is to love each other, embrace each other fully for who you are, including the faults and quirks and feelings. It is okay to be human. If you take a risk you will feel good about yourself for stretching. *Wow, that took a lot of courage, that was pretty brave of me. I wouldn't have told that to anybody else in a million years and you know what? I'm not going to tell that to anybody else, but I'm so glad I shared that with my partner, because we are now closer, we are more strongly connected, and it reinforces for me that I can be fully who I am here in this relationship.*

If you wait for it to be comfortable or put it off until "the time is right," it's not going to happen.

If you are willing to put yourself out there, you will be always stretching yourself, growing the relationship, and experiencing excitement. If you play it safe, you won't. Remember, feeling a little fear is okay. Leaving your comfort zone will be scary. It's never going to be easy. If you wait for it to be comfortable or put it off until "the time is right," it's not going to happen. To develop *Radical Intimacy*, you must *continually take risks.*

Radical Action:

Next time you catch yourself having a thought, feeling, need, fantasy or desire and not sharing it with your partner, make a conscious effort to share it anyway. Watch how often you censor yourself and try to take risks by sharing everything with your partner, no matter how trivial or embarrassing.

Radical Intimacy Strategy #4: Rituals

You and your partner must build regular times into your routine to be present together and share what's inside you. This can include daily ten-minute check-ins over coffee or dinner, or sitting down after the kids are in bed. This can also include blocks of time on the weekend for a date or a do-it-yourself retreat, which we highly recommend. This strategy was discussed in *Radical Communication* and it will be further explored in *radical romance,* but it's also applicable in *Radical Intimacy.*

The Relationship Journal described in Chapter Five is an excellent way to open the floodgates of communication by taking a fun, deliberate step toward sharing your deepest thoughts and desires with your partner. You will appreciate the effort from them and they will appreciate the effort from you. You can make it a special and regular event, complete with rituals, where you clear the decks and let into your lives a rush of honesty, compassion and connection as a way of deepening intimacy.

A wonderful way to bring more intimacy into your life is through rituals.

Rituals are routines in your relationship that you both know when, where, and how they're going to happen. It's like getting up in the morning and going to bed at night, or putting on your socks or brushing your teeth—it's just a regular part of your day. In this case, it's a regular part of your relationship. The wonderful thing about rituals is that you can create them. They tie into the fun part of a relationship where you get to make it up as you go. You can design new rituals all the time, and those rituals can change. If one gets boring, and you don't want to do it anymore, you can shake things up. A great relationship requires intimacy, and a wonderful way to bring more intimacy into your life is through *rituals.*

Radical Action:

> If you haven't already, co-create a daily connection ritual with your partner when you will check in about your day (what happened outside of you), your experience (what happened inside of you), and a current need or desire. Though it might be challenging when you have a busy lifestyle, this is the single best thing you can do for your relationship.

Radical Intimacy Strategy #5: Text Messaging

Text messaging is a concept that can be accomplished with paper and pencil or through electronic means. The point, here, is to regularly write your partner spontaneous love notes or convey little ideas, thoughts, feelings, wants and needs. Sometimes it's easier and more convenient to text your most intimate thoughts and feelings as they occur to you and then talk about them later. While you are thinking about your partner and something occurs to you that you'd like to share with them, go ahead and text them. Write to them right then and there about what's on your mind and expand upon your thoughts when time allows.

Texting is an intimate activity.

Texting is an intimate activity, and we are aware of at least two mobile apps built around it for couples to share a direct connection. One is called Couple, and another is WeSync. We have tried them and we like them both. They work well and they are private. Communication takes place just between you and your partner, with no intermediary. It's like having a hotline for your relationship available any time of the day.

A Radical Marriage requires emotional maturity, self-knowledge, and a willingness to openly communicate. If you're looking for a fantastic strategy for doing that, for maintaining and deepening your relationship through Radical Intimacy, try *text messaging*.

Radical Action:

Send your partner a message (text, email, voicemail, etc) at least once per day about something you'd like to share or talk about later during your connection ritual. This will let them know you're thinking of them and will promote closeness, connection and intimacy even when you're apart.

Radical Intimacy Strategy #6: Telling the Whole Truth

There is much more to your truth than just one sentence.

There is often more to your truth than what you are consciously aware. To deepen the intimacy you share with your partner, you must allow more of your truth to emerge. Peel away more layers of the onion. Chances are there is much more to your truth than just one sentence. Take a sentence that is truthful and expand that into a paragraph. The more truth you share, the more truth emerges. Likely, you can expand that paragraph into a whole page. Going further, there is often more there and you can share more pages, and so on, until it's all out and there is nothing more. If you want Radical Intimacy, you must give yourself time, dig deep, and practice *Telling the Whole Truth.*

Radical Action:

During your connection ritual when you're sharing a thought, feeling, need or desire, take the time to share even more about it. What does this mean to you? Where does it come from? What's your experience of having it and not having it? What's it connected to? Why is it coming up now? Dig down and share all there is you can find, until it's all out on the table for your partner to share with you.

Radical Intimacy Strategy #7: Reinforce Commitment

To deepen intimacy with your partner, it's helpful to continually remind yourself and your partner in words and behavior that you're not going anywhere, no matter what. That is our very definition of commitment. As we discussed in Chapter Two, in a committed relationship there are no exits. Problems are to be solved and worked out, rather than reasons for leaving the relationship. If you feel safe in your commitment with each other then you are not going anywhere. You can share anything. You can be fully who you are and feel safe doing so. You can remind each other that it is safe, and that you're staying put.

We all need reassurance sometimes.

We all need reassurance sometimes. We need to know that we're loved. The more it is expressed in your words and behavior, the safer and more comfortable you will feel to tell your truth, and even be *aware* of what your truth is to tell your partner. It's an important part of a fulfilling relationship. Knowing that you and your partner are here to stay, no matter what, enhances your intimacy by enhancing your *commitment*.

Radical Action:

Every once in a while, no less than once per month, share with your partner how much you love them, how grateful you are to be married to them, how they enhance your life, how you're looking forward to growing old together; really pour it on and (truthfully) gush about how wonderful they are and how lucky you feel to have them in your life. Not only will they feel wonderful and appreciated and loved and more connected with you, but you will have a heightened appreciation for your partner and your marriage and won't be at risk for taking them for granted.

144

Radical Intimacy Strategy #8: Positive Response

*This doesn't mean you have to agree with them or
that they must be exactly the same as yours.*

To be radically intimate with your partner is to respond with acceptance, embracing and supporting all of your partner's thoughts, feelings, wants, needs, secrets, fantasies, and desires. This doesn't mean you have to agree with them or that they must be exactly the same as yours. And it doesn't mean that you must support something that doesn't really work for you. If your partner has a fantasy of polygamy, it doesn't mean that you have to actually do it. But you can allow them to have that fantasy and even role-play and have fun with it.

Generally, as previously mentioned, a positive response means that you never say "no." Instead, you identify what you *can* do. And it doesn't always have to do with sex or relationship-type ideas. If your partner wants to parachute out of an airplane at 10,000 feet and you just can't see yourself doing that, that's okay. Rather than say, "No way, I'm not doing that," perhaps you can find something you can say "yes" to. "Well, I don't know if you're aware of it, but there's this cool technology nowadays where we can go to a place and walk into a padded room and there are huge fans that blow upward and we can get the sensation of experiencing parachuting. It's indoors, it's safe, and we're no more than ten feet off the ground. How about that?"

There are always ways to make it work if you have a positive attitude and give a positive response. It's what draws us closer and strengthens our connection. If you put something out to your partner and you know you're not going to be rejected or judged, then life together becomes more intimate. It doesn't mean you're going to get everything you want. You're an adult. You can handle it. Just because you want a basket full of candy doesn't mean you're going to get a basket full of candy. Still, it's nice to be positively received, really responded to, and building a Radical Marriage through Radical Intimacy.

The important aspect here is to support your partner to be who they are, help them express who they are, and allow them to have whatever fantasies, desires, secrets, wants, needs, feelings and thoughts they have. It's all okay. There is no wrong. Your job is to provide a *positive response*.

Radical Action:

Commit to your partner that your intention is to never say "No" and request that they remind you of this commitment if you slip up (and you will slip up!).

Radical Intimacy Strategy #9: Self-Management

It is critical in a relationship to take responsibility for your own reactions when your partner triggers your fears, insecurities, negative feelings, or judgments. Remember, any time you have a judgment, it's about you. It's your opinion and your story about it. You may think horror movies are bad and scary and you may not understand why they are entertaining to others and why anybody would want to watch them, but your partner may love horror movies. Your judgment about horror movies is all about you. You can detest horror movies and still support your partner in enjoying them.

---

*Practicing non-judgment does not mean
you don't have judgments.*

You own all of your reactions, and rest assured you're going to have them. Practicing non-judgment does not mean you don't have judgments, it means that you take responsibility for and manage the ones you have. They belong to you, and you must acknowledge that. You don't make your partner wrong, and say, "How can you like that movie? That's a ridiculous movie, that's a

146

terrible movie. I don't want to see that movie, and I don't understand how you could want to see that movie."

Self-management also means that when you have an *emotion*, like anger, fear, anxiety, resentment, or whatever else is going on inside you, that you take responsibility for that. It's not your partner's fault. Granted, this is a hard one for a lot of people, because emotion is very strong. It triggers all sorts of chemicals in the body, and it really does seem like your partner is the cause for this. They aren't. You could have the very same experience with somebody else who wasn't your partner and you could simply ignore it and it wouldn't be a big deal to you.

Let's say your partner farts. You feel disgust and repulsion. You have your judgment and your reaction. "How dare you!" If you were somewhere else and a baby farted, you might be amused or think, *How cute!* or *No big deal, people fart.* In a relationship, though, we tend to hold our partner to a higher standard, and it's not fair. We need to take responsibility for our thoughts, feelings, wants, needs, issues, judgments, and fears, because they belong to us. We need to be honest about that.

When you have negative reactions, you need to catch yourself. "Oops, that was about me, not about you, sweetheart." It takes practice and it can seem unnatural. Eventually, if you're in a committed, authentic, intimate relationship, you will come to a place where you are so evolved and so serene, that people can do whatever they're going to do and you'll just let it be.

It's not about you. Realize that, and you will have mastered *self-management*.

Radical Action:

Practice ownership in your communication by prefacing your statements by labeling what they are. For example, "I feel…." "I judge…," "I want…," "I need…," "My opinion is…," etc. This will help your communication be clean and honest, and enhance your conscious awareness to be able to successfully manage any reactivity.

Radical Intimacy Strategy #10: Push Your Upper Limit

Getting radical in your intimacy goes hand in hand with allowing yourself to dream beyond what you think is realistic. You must catch and challenge yourself by asking, *What else? What am I holding back? What do I really want?*

We all have an upper limit, the threshold beyond which we feel uncomfortable being happy, just like we all have a lower limit, the threshold beyond which we can't take any more pain. Believe it or not, there is such a thing as too much happiness, and when we reach that self-defined upper limit, we tend to sabotage ourselves and bring ourselves down to a more comfortable level. The challenge in a relationship is to constantly push your upper limit to allow yourself to experience increasing levels of intimacy, happiness, and fulfillment, because it's hard to fight your natural tendency.

Think about the level of intimacy that you were able to handle when you were dating, or when you were a teenager, or when you were in your twenties. It's not the same level of intimacy that you're ready for, available for, and able to handle when you're older and more mature, or when a relationship has matured.

Pushing your upper limit means allowing yourself to dream beyond what you think is realistic.

Pushing your upper limit means allowing yourself to dream beyond what you think is realistic. When you catch yourself holding back, challenge yourself by asking those important questions: *What else? What am I holding back? What do I really want?* Most of us especially benefit from the *What do I really want?* question because it can be hard to allow ourselves to have or be in touch with what we want. We must ask ourselves, *What do I REALLY want?*

If you want to go out to dinner, it's not enough to ask, *What do I want to eat?* Chances are there are fifty things you would like to eat. When you ask, *What do I really want?* you have to dig deeper and determine what would excite you. Then you begin to realize what would really turn you on and make you happy.

Note that what you want can change. It's not going to be the same thing every time. But *What do I really want?* is a great question that we invite you to ask yourself regularly as a way of pushing your upper limit and going beyond your normal routine. This is about having a *Radical Marriage, Radical Living*, and experiencing *Radical Intimacy*. To do that, you must *push your upper limit.*

So, as you seek more fulfillment in your relationship and marriage, peel away those layers of the onion. Keep on sharing your whole truth. Keep on asking, *What else?* until there is nothing more. Lay it all out there. Ask yourself, *What am I holding back? What do I really want?*

We all hold things back from time to time;
it's unconscious.

We all hold things back from time to time; it's unconscious. When we were kids we would get in trouble if we did or said what we really wanted to do or say. As a result, we became conditioned to stay safe. As adults we need to unlearn that. We need to take risks and allow ourselves to bring forth the truths, wants, needs, fantasies, desires, and secrets that we would ordinarily suppress.

Radical Action:

When you're faced with making a choice (where to eat, what to do, etc) practice asking yourself "What do I *really* want?" Be honest with yourself and don't allow yourself to be passive, apathetic, settle for less, be "realistic" or acquiesce (even to your partner) to be "nice." Don't avoid conflict unless you *want* to defer to your partner's happiness, but don't make doing so a recurring habit, which would be an unconscious pattern instead of a conscious choice. Counter the pattern of deferring to your partner by continually asking yourself "What do I *really* want?"

Summary of Radical Intimacy Strategies

Strategy #1: Create safety for yourself
Strategy #2: Create safety for your partner
Strategy #3: Continually take risks
Strategy #4: Rituals
Strategy #5: Text messaging
Strategy #6: Telling the whole truth
Strategy #7: Reinforce your commitment
Strategy #8: Positive response
Strategy #9: Self-management
Strategy #10: Push your upper limit

While they're not for everybody, these ten strategies for Radical Intimacy can put you on the path to Radical Marriage by stoking the adventure in your life with your partner. They will help you explore the deep reaches of inner and outer relationship space, going beyond where no other couple has gone before to a place of fulfillment that you can only go with your partner through *Radical Intimacy*.

Chapter Eight: Radical Romance

When looking for ways to get outside the norm and intensify the romance in your relationship, it's important to first understand a couple of important words. The first is *love*, the other is *romance*.

The dictionary defines *love* as "a profoundly tender, passionate affection for another person." So, love is a *feeling*, an involuntary emotion that happens inside you.

Romance, however, means "to court or woo with ardor." So, romance is an *action*, a conscious choice.

Radical Romance is a term we coined that means to energetically, creatively, and continuously express your love and woo your partner. It's something that often happens by itself early in a relationship but tends to fade away over time. Couples become comfortable with each other and complacent, and their relationship drifts into the boring, stale, and routine.

Routines can also become suffocating and boring.
We need excitement and variety as well.

We all fall into routines in relationships, and there is nothing inherently wrong with that. Routines are comforting and make life as a couple run smoothly. But routines can also become suffocating and boring. We need excitement and variety as well.

So how can you spice up your love life with Radical Romance? There are three requirements: a radical marriage attitude, radical marriage actions, and radical marriage strategies.

Radical Marriage Attitude

Radical Marriage Attitude means you strive to be the best partner you can be and co-create the exciting, fun, fulfilling relationship that you and your partner both want. An attitude is a point of view. It's a belief system. It's where you are coming from in your head. It's the way you think about things. It's your lens or filter for the world.

You might notice that some people have an attitude in a relationship that is entitled, like, "I deserve to be happy and it's my partner's job to make me happy," or codependent, such as "Well, I don't really deserve love, so it's my job to take care of my partner and love them so they'll love me back." That's not the state of mind we're looking for here. No, a good, healthy, strong attitude in a relationship exists when each of you take 100% responsibility for your outcomes in the relationship.

Radical Marriage Action

Radical Marriage Action means you take initiative and responsibility by doing things with and for your partner every day that enhance your relationship and your life together.

We're not kidding about this.

Every day we have many opportunities to do things for our partner and make our partner happy.

Every day we have many opportunities to do things for our partner and make our partner happy, from the moment we get up until the time we go to bed at night. How you show up in a relationship, every day, either expresses your love to your partner or it does not. It either expresses the value you place on the relationship or it does not. Imagine what your marriage would be like if you worked every day to make it the best marriage possible.

Radical Marriage Strategy

Radical Marriage Strategy means that you think ahead and come up with specific ideas about how you can improve your life together as a couple. It means you have a *radical attitude*, you are willing to take the *radical action*, and you *plan and follow through* on your promises to fulfill your Radical Marriage. To do that, you must get creative and dedicate your time and efforts to go beyond happily ever after. As an example, let's expand upon a wonderful and proven process. It's one that we have previously discussed, is effective in several areas, and ties nicely into *Radical Romance*. We're talking about the Relationship Journal.

Using The Relationship Journal for Radical Romance

Romance requires intention,
and it's a requirement in any good relationship.

Romance requires intention, and it's a requirement in any good relationship. *Radical Romance,* on the other hand, is about taking that intention to the next level. It requires making a special effort beyond the norm to transport your marriage beyond happily ever after. One of our all-time favorite tools for this is the *Relationship Journal.* As we have mentioned, it is something that was originally created to help a struggling relationship. Since then, it has evolved and been adapted into the context of a Radical Marriage, and when combined with the added element of a relationship retreat, it epitomizes the concept of *Radical Romance*.

Your Radical Marriage Retreat

While the basic principles are the same—discovering, presenting, and solving issues through using the Relationship Journal—the added romance comes in breaking away from the confines of everyday life. Rather than just committing to a scheduled place and time, make the effort to really spice it up and make it special.

Reserve a nice, seaside house for a weekend or head up into the mountains. If you live inland or are unable to travel too far, perhaps you can find a lake or a cozy place that you both agree would be a wonderful retreat.

This alone is often enough to bring out your romantic side, and a sign that you are both willing to work to strengthen your relationship. In addition to some valuable relaxation, reflection, and whatever else strikes your fancy, you will also spend your time full of intention. You and your partner will identify what you need, any potential issues and how to address them, and consciously and effectively co-create your relationship and lives together.

It's important to create an intimate space when pursuing this path. Remember, this is a ritual, and as a ritual you should do things to stage it as such. You might start by putting on the teakettle for tea. Light a candle. Turn off the ringer on the telephone. Put on soft music. Turn down the lights. Whatever it is that will help you get where you need to be. These will serve as visual cues to get you and your partner in the proper mindset.

Dealing with Resistance

If, however, you have taken the initiative to create an intimate space and invited your partner into it, and they don't want to do it, then what you have is a resistant partner. You have some work to do to cultivate your *Radical Romance*. Remember, this is about consciously co-creating your relationship. Both you and your partner must take responsibility for doing it, and you both have an obligation to show up, physically, mentally, and spiritually.

This is not to say that things might not ever come up that prevent your partner from accepting the invitation or showing up when it's time for action. If you are having trouble pinning your partner down and they have a problem keeping their agreements, the Relationship Journal may not necessarily solve the real problem. Still, this strategy will enable you to bring some things out into the open to where you are able to be much more conscious, instead of reactive, about what is going on in the relationship. It truly is a wonderful process, in and of itself, and if you can get your partner alone on a romantic retreat, you will increase the likelihood that your relationship can derive maximum benefit from it.

The Relationship Journal facilitates dialogue,
and when conducted as part of a getaway,
heightens your romantic energy.

The Relationship Journal facilitates dialogue, and when conducted as part of a getaway, heightens your romantic energy. When you write in your journal you are contemplating what's going on for you and discovering what your truth is. Sometimes it can be a lot harder to do that when you're engaged with your partner. When you are engaged with yourself, writing, you can tap into a whole new area of thought and explore new areas of yourself that don't emerge in everyday life. Writing takes you places you never knew you could go—you write something, and then something else comes up, and something else comes up. It's a whole lot easier to get in touch with your deepest truth that way.

Some people, however, as we explored in *Radical Communication*, are more verbal. They need to talk about it. They need to think out loud. And some people are more introverted and they need to go inside first to get at what their truth is. Writing in a journal is a way of communicating or discovering something that might be harder to communicate or get in touch with regarding what is true and real for you.

Dealing with Reactivity

Earlier in our emotional, psychological, and relational development, we have more difficulty accepting differences and things that threaten our ego. We get defensive. But sometimes even good or evolved marriages tend to fall victim to bad habits. The Relationship Journal is a useful tool for communicating things that would ordinarily create reactivity like defensiveness, anger, or

156

frustration. It's a forum where you and your partner can write about things in a controlled environment, free from distractions and away from the ordinary. Then you can read what each other wrote, giving it due process and full consideration without any sidebars.

Coping with Interruptions

One of the problems or bad habits couples run into when communicating is they interrupt each other. The Relationship Journal helps you express yourself in complete thoughts without being interrupted, which helps the flow as you are conveying your issues, needs, and desires to your partner, as well as sharing what you appreciate about them.

When people are interrupted, they feel misunderstood. They can't go back and recapture the thought they were working on or the mood that they were in before. As a result, in discussing issues, people often walk away dissatisfied. Writing allows you to take your time, fully develop your thoughts, get more deeply in touch with your feelings, and clearly express what you want to say, which is crucial to deepening your connection.

Process vs. Content

---

*You can't deal with the content
if the process isn't working.*

In understanding the Relationship Journal, it is important to highlight the distinction between process and content. *Content* refers to the information that you are communicating and *process* refers to the way in which you communicate. If your partner chimes in or reacts when you are speaking then that interrupts the transmission of your content, which prevents the process from working. You can't deal with the content if the process isn't working.

The Relationship Journal provides structure—in this case on a romantic getaway—to foster a productive process so that you can deal with the content. But despite your best intentions sometimes things don't go as planned, even on vacation. If you and your partner find yourselves arguing and disagreeing, angry and frustrated, then the process is intercepting the content and interfering with the relationship. Your communication, then, is no longer about the content or your need, it's about how the process, and the communication between you and your partner is no longer working.

Communication breakdown often happens with young couples and in relationships that are under-developed, but it also occasionally creeps into more established relationships. Sometimes when we have been together for a while we get lazy and take things for granted. Despite a certain developmental maturity in a relationship—where we can talk about things that might have been difficult for us to hear ten or twenty years ago, accepting and tolerating differences—sometimes an unstructured process can bring out the worst in us. Radical Romance is not settling for the norm or default; it's about rekindling that fire, bringing out our best, and going beyond happily ever after.

The Bridge to Connection

The Relationship Journal is a helpful way to bridge any immaturities, bad habits, or difficulties in communicating with your partner. Having a writing process is a wonderful way to work things out and consciously co-create a relationship. Yes, you could communicate with the help of a third party—a counselor, therapist, or mentor—and there's nothing wrong with that; we advocate doing it. But the journaling process is a wonderful self-coaching process, and we recommend it for all couples.

A good agreement is one that both partners can keep.

The Relationship Journal is not reserved for broken agreements or apparent issues. It can be used in any relationship, at any point, at any time. The key is that you must have a desire to co-create your relationship, consciously, and take your relationship to the next level. Remember, if an agreement is not kept then it was a bad agreement in the first place. A good agreement is one that both partners can keep.

There are many ways to meet a need. If one or both of you have trouble keeping an agreement, then it must have not been effective in the first place. Work to come up with something that really works for both of you. "I have an issue that's recurring and we had an agreement last time about this, but it wasn't kept. I'm not going to take issue with you breaking the agreement, but I still have an unmet need here." The next time you use the Relationship Journal together your goal will be to revisit the agreement and work something out—refine it, revise it, change it—so that it's more effective.

Solving Unsolvable Problems

Let us remind you that there is such a thing as an unsolvable problem. But even that shouldn't leave your hands tied. There are four ways to "solve" an unsolvable problem:

1. You can live with it and be unhappy, which is a valid option because problems don't stay the same and it just might go away on its own.

2. You can leave the relationship or leave the problem in certain ways, like avoiding your partner during certain times or circumstances.

3. You can negotiate the problem, or compromise, in which case you're not getting 100% of what you want. This means the problem isn't really going to be "solved" as you're meeting in the middle. You're doing what you can about it. Despite the problem becoming more *livable* for you, it hasn't necessarily gone away.

4. You can let go of the problem. Sometimes this is possible to do, especially in an area of growth for you. For example, let's say it's an issue for you every time your partner looks at an attractive person of the opposite sex. It makes you jealous and insecure. When you bring it up during the Relationship Journal, you come up with agreements. "Okay, I won't look at anybody of the opposite sex, ever." That's a hard agreement to keep. Well, then "How about, I won't look at *attractive* people of the opposite sex." That's a hard one to keep, too. Hmm, "I know, I won't look at attractive people for more than a *nanosecond*." Also hard to keep. So, you keep on trying to solve this unsolvable problem. *How in the world can you get somebody to not look at anybody that you don't want them to look at?* It's nearly impossible.

---

*It is possible for you to let go of the problem
and take responsibility.*

True, it may be impossible for you to prevent somebody's behavior, but it *is* possible for you to let go of the problem and take responsibility. *Maybe I'm just being insecure and I'm being jealous and this is about me. They don't need to be doing anything differently. When I experience the issue, this is something that I need to take care of.*

Dealing with Unmet Requirements

Some things that are unsolvable are related to unmet requirements like, say, infidelity. Obviously, if you require monogamy and your partner sleeps around, it will cause some pain. If you talk about it, talk about it, talk about it; make agreements, make agreements, make agreements; and the pacts are broken, broken, broken, then it's a major problem. Do you really want to stick around and continue that relationship?

*If you've reached the end of your rope, and you've done
everything you can on your own in a relationship,
then it's time to get some help.*

There are times when you must take an unsolvable problem and get professional support for it. If you've reached the end of your rope, and you've done everything you can on your own in a relationship, then it's time to get some help. Sometimes you can take care of things on your own, but there comes a point, in spite of all your individual efforts, where an unsolvable problem is getting in the way of you moving forward together. At that point, you should seek the assistance of a professional.

Reconnecting

The Relationship Journal is a great way to reconnect with your partner. Even if you have a great relationship you can feel as though you are sliding into a rut. In this case it is helpful to take some time away, go on a nice, romantic retreat, and have a process for reconnecting.

When you are reconnecting it can be helpful to be conscious of not only the differences in styles of communication, but also the common, if not stereotypical disparity between genders.

Dealing with Gender Differences

As David will be the first to tell you, sometimes guys are more comfortable having instructions to follow—even if the ladies feel that they are not very good at it—than trying to read between the lines or pick up signals. In that regard, the Relationship Journal acts as a facilitator to get the ball rolling.

Though we can't speak for everyone, we imagine that most guys would be more comfortable having a tool of some kind. Guys like tools. For them, having tools is easier than sitting down face-to-face and just talking in an unstructured manner. Most guys would hate it if they were approached with, "Honey, would you please just sit down and tell me how you feel?" That's kind of a guy's nightmare. Most men would feel more comfortable with a process than with something less structured.

Introducing the Relationship Journal

All relationships, no matter how good,
have things that could be improved.

A great way to introduce the Relationship Journal to your partner is to just ask them to review this section of the book with you. Another is to just simply get a couple of blank notebooks, sit down with your partner, and ask them if they are willing to be proactive and participate in a process to improve your relationship. Again, this is not necessarily because there is anything wrong. It's because all relationships, no matter how good, have things that could be improved. *Remember: We are talking about beyond* happily ever after. We are talking about a *Radical Marriage*. The idea is to always be improving and strengthening your relationship.

As we mentioned earlier, this concept was started as a self-guided relationship retreat. This is where the *Radical Romance* comes in. We do recommend renting a place for a weekend or at least getting away from all distractions to allow yourselves to spend some quality time together, focusing on the Relationship Journal, going through the process, and co-creating your relationship. Take a moment and really imagine what it would be like for you and your partner to do that. Most partners interested in developing a Radical Marriage would be open to it.

It Takes Two

The relationship takes two, improving a relationship takes two, romance takes two, and the Relationship Journal takes two. If your partner absolutely refuses, and it could happen, our best recommendation is to be patient. Nothing stays the same. Things change. Things evolve. That's what we know. Right now, your partner might refuse to take part for whatever reason, and we don't really even need to know why. What we can hang on to is that they won't feel the exact same way or think the same thoughts in a week, month, or year from now. Guaranteed.

Remember, if your physical safety isn't at risk, there is no such thing as a relationship emergency. Although it feels urgent—you may be upset, really want to talk it out and long to come up with a solution—the reality is that you must be patient. You might have to let it ride for a while. In that case, you can do your thing, cool down, live your life, and address it together when the time is better.

Positive Intent

Now, you may wonder if approaching your partner about the Relationship Journal could initiate fear within them that you think the relationship is damaged or hurting. Approaching it as a retreat can help with this as it demonstrates your passion and desire to get away with your partner and deepen your relationship. Approach your partner with positive intent and say, "Honey, I love you. Our relationship is good, and I want to make it even better. Would you be willing to participate in a process that might help do that?"

The Relationship Journal is not about diagnosing what's wrong or determining who's at fault or trying to fix something. It's about having an intention and a vision for what you want to create in your relationship, setting goals for accomplishing that vision, and taking action toward accomplishing your goals. That's *Radical Romance*, and that's why we love coaching. It's positive, conscious, and action-oriented. Most partners would respond favorably to a genuine statement of love and positive action.

Dealing with Getting Stuck

If, however, you are in a bad place, and your partner is stuck in resentment, then they may be more invested in defending themselves. They're hurting, they're angry, and when this happens, you basically have two choices: You can be patient or you can get help from a facilitator in the hopes that they can break the log jam.

When a person is stuck, angry, and unapproachable,
they tend to need space.

In our experience, when a person is stuck, angry, and unapproachable, they tend to need space. Don't push your partner. Be patient. In the end, it's important to get your partner to understand what your need is, that it's a real need, and that you are not just trying to force them to change. Remember the Communication Map. Identifying a need is a problem-solving process. It's like doing your taxes. "Here's the box. What goes in this box?" With a relationship it's, "Here's the issue. What is the need that must be met so this issue will go away?" It's simply dealing with information and data. Having it in writing adds more objectivity than talking about it face-to-face. That's the beauty of the Relationship Journal.

Dealing with Defensiveness

The Relationship Journal helps deal with a defensive partner because you are writing it out. It's a non-blaming process. Blaming merely serves to make a partner feel responsible for a problem, which is inefficient in getting needs met. No matter the issue, writing things out and following the Relationship Journal process is more helpful than just confronting your partner. First you begin with what you appreciate about your partner, and then write out any issues that you're experiencing. This is where it becomes important to focus on facts.

As a reminder, a fact is an actual event. It's something that happened. It's inarguable. Your issue can't be, "You behaved like a jerk last night." That's a judgment. That's an opinion. That's an accusation. A fact is, "You ate all the ice cream last night and didn't offer me any." That actually happened. Focusing on facts helps you get to the root of the need.

Again, if neither writing nor talking face-to-face is working, then please do get the support you need. Don't stay stuck. There's no reason to languish in misery and continue something that's not working. We're not saying you should break it off because it's not working; We're saying you should assume it can be solved and not accept that it has to continue to be problematic. Be proactive. Get the support you need.

Radical Marriage Dates

In addition to breaking away for a romantic weekend retreat with the Relationship Journal, there is another way you can weave more romance into your regular routine. It comes back to an activity that once got your heart pumping and that will still do it today as you develop your Radical Marriage, applying what you've learned in *Radical Commitment*, *Radical Communication*, and *Radical Intimacy*, and now incorporating *Radical Romance*. It's the exciting act of courtship we call *radical dates*.

---

*Dating, while obviously important as you are starting
and ramping up your relationship,
is often overlooked once a couple is married.*

Dating, while obviously important as you are starting and ramping up your relationship, is often overlooked once a couple is married. Long ago used as a way to get to know and woo a potential partner, it tends to fade into the category of ancient history. When you are married and your relationship has fallen into mediocrity, we recommend getting radical by dusting off some of the activities that helped stoke your passion and fall in love in the first place.

One-Way Dates

As mentioned earlier, couples often fall into compromise traps where each gives up what they really want to find something they both can agree upon. This is especially true for dates. A better way to go is to negotiate, where you come up with a solution that meets both of your needs. But, whether it's watching a movie or getting romantic, it's rare that you get to have the kind of experience that you really want, so we have devised a strategy for doing so, and it centers on four types of one-way dates.

Type One Dates: Create a Romantic Experience for Your Partner

Type One Dates are those in which you create a romantic experience for your partner. The focus is exclusively on them and making them happy and creating the romantic experience of their dreams, without thought of what you want or prefer. It is absolutely 100% for your partner.

Type Two Dates: Your Partner Creates a Romantic Experience for You

Type Two Dates are those in which you switch, and your partner creates a romantic experience for you. They put their creativity and effort and energy into creating a romantic experience that would make you ecstatically happy without thought of whether they would want to do it or not. It's totally for you.

Type Three Dates: Create a Romantic Experience for Yourself

Type Three Dates are created as a self-centered romantic experience. This is where you create the romantic experience of your dreams, for yourself, that you want to share with your partner. Your partner is a supporting player in your date, but you have the lead role. You get to have it exactly the way you want it.

Type Four Dates: Your Partner Creates a Romantic Experience for Their Self

Type Four Dates are a reversal of Type Three Dates. In Type Four Dates your partner creates a self-centered romantic experience for themselves and you are the supporting player. Your job is to go along and to help them have a good time, to help them have the fulfilling, romantic experience that they really want and that they created for themselves. You hate the opera; they love the opera. You're going to the opera and you're going to be happy to go because it makes you happy to make your partner happy.

Suggestions

To make things run smoothly for these four types of dates, there are a number of things that you can do. Here are some suggestions:

Co-create it

Discuss and commit on the plan together. This is not something that we recommend that you do by yourself. You could create an experience for your partner 100% without them doing it for you. You could create an experience for yourself 100% and ask them to play along. But this plan works *much* better when you are co-creating it, when you are teaming up. Both of you are doing this, so discuss and commit to the plan together.

Schedule it

Get your calendar out and schedule them months or even a year in advance.

Make sure to schedule your one-way dates. Get your calendar out and schedule them months or even a year in advance, so that you

167

both know when to expect them and you have the time blocked out.

We also recommend designating the type of date for each date on your calendar. You might start off with Type One followed by Type Two, Type Three, and Type Four. Then, next month, start over again. This way, when the date approaches you both know what kind of date it is and whose responsibility it is to put the time and energy into creating the experience for that date.

Plan it

For this dating system to work you must plan your dates ahead of time. Do not wait until the last minute. Your partner will be disappointed. This plan works best when you put some time looking into the future rather than waiting for the last minute, struggling to find something to do. Remember: This is about *Radical Romance*, which requires a quality experience, which requires intent, which requires forethought. So, at least a week before your scheduled date, think about it and put some plans in place for exactly what you are going to do on that date.

Own it

Don't compromise. Own what you want. These are *one-way* dates. If you try to come up with a romantic experience for yourself that you think is acceptable to your partner, you're compromising. If you try to come up with a romantic experience for your partner that you can live with, you're compromising. This strategy works best when you are absolutely designing the romantic experience of your dreams for yourself or of your partner's dreams for them, without censoring, without compromising.

Make each date unique. Don't recycle past dates.

We also recommend that you make each date unique. Don't recycle past dates, even if you had a great time and you would love to do it again. When you do that, you develop a routine, and that's what we are trying to get away from here.

Keep it

You must make every effort to keep your agreements. A relationship is based upon trust with respect to just about everything, whether it's money or kids or chores. Your entire life together is based on agreements. For your one-way dates and your *Radical Romance* you must first discuss a plan and set the dates, and then you *must* keep those agreements, which means you must have a good agreement from the start.

If the date and time comes around and you forgot about it or you didn't prepare, then you will have broken the agreement, and the plan won't work. If you do that consistently, your relationship won't work either.

Budget it

Definitely discuss your time investment with each other. How much time can you devote to this? Is it going to be a two-hour experience, a four-day experience, a weekend experience? Budget your money as well. Most people have limited funds. They're not able to spend an unlimited amount of money on these experiences, and really, you don't need to spend any money on them. Set agreements around how much time and money to spend on your one-way dates as you cultivate *Radical Romance*.

Enjoy it

In creating a fulfilling experience for your partner, if you have anything less than a positive attitude, they will not have the experience that they deserve, and vice versa; after all, they want you to have a good time, too. Think about it: Can you really have fun knowing that your partner is just gritting their teeth and getting through it? You must have a positive attitude for each date.

Scratch it

---

*Don't plan a date based on what your partner did the last time.
Start each date from scratch.*

Don't try to one-up your partner. Don't play tit for tat. Don't plan a date based on what your partner did the last time. Start each date from scratch, with a blank slate. Don't keep score. A relationship doesn't work well if you keep score and your one-way dates won't work well either. Sometimes one-way is the best way in a successful relationship.

So have fun, make the most of The Relationship Journal and your new "one-way" approach to dating, and get creative with *Radical Romance*.

Summary of Radical Romance (One-Way) Dates

Type One: Create a romantic experience for your partner

Type Two: Your partner creates a romantic experience for you

Type Three: Create a romantic experience for yourself

Type Four: Your partner creates a romantic experience for you

Chapter Nine: Radical Sex

In introducing the concept of beyond happily ever after and laying the foundation for Radical Marriage, we have detailed some critical concepts along the way: *Radical Commitment, Radical Communication, Radical Intimacy, and Radical Romance*. The next logical step gets us into *Radical Sex*, and it starts with a few questions.

What kind of sexual relationship do you want? Daily sex? Sex whenever you want? Adventurous sex? Slow, sensuous, erotic sex? Emotionally and spiritually connected sex? Do you want extraordinary sex but don't know how to get your partner on board? What would make you radically, ecstatically happy with your sex life beyond your wildest dreams?

As a way of helping you explore the possibilities for your sex life, we have broken this important topic into two sections: Part 1 covers seven foundational "good" sex strategies that can apply to all couples, and Part 2 covers seven Radical Sex strategies that go beyond what most couples experience.

The Truth about Sex

Sex is a huge driver in relationships. It's a strong, natural human desire built into our body. It pulls people together and drives us apart. When it works it's wonderful, and most couples value monogamy and fidelity. But when our sex life doesn't work, many turn to affairs and many of those relationships end in divorce.

We are all sexual beings and a satisfying sexual relationship is an important bond that helps couples live happily ever after, and beyond. Sex in a new relationship is almost always exciting, but sex in a long-term relationship can become routine and boring. After people have been together for a while they find themselves doing the same thing, the same way, every time.

While routine can be comforting and enjoyable,
most people need variety to keep things fresh.

Getting bored with things is a common feeling. If you love chocolate ice cream, and you eat it every day, it eventually loses its appeal. It's the same with your sex life. While routine can be comforting and enjoyable, most people need variety to keep things fresh. What's more, partners have different and ever-changing sexual wants, needs, and desires. So, as important as sex is, with all its complexities and differences, it's a wonder that relationships work at all.

Here's the good news: Sex in a long-term relationship can be even more exciting and fulfilling than sex in a new relationship. Yes, it takes a while to get to know your partner, but when you do you will be amazed how fulfilling your sex life can be. You must give yourself time to fully understand your partner's response to different touches, sexual wants and needs, and turn-ons and turn-offs.

Practice makes perfect, and the longer you and your partner are together, the more sexual experiences you can have, and the better the sex can be. It's a reciprocal relationship. You need trust, intimacy, commitment, and communication for great sex; and great sex strengthens trust, intimacy, commitment, and communication.

Regular Sex vs. Radical Sex

If you think about it, you will see that the secret to a fulfilling sex life can be distilled down to a few simple parts. In fact, it's the same winning formula for finding general happiness in a relationship.

Take a walk to your favorite park, catch a movie, or grab a bite to eat and you will notice the full spectrum of couples. You will notice people who are new to the relationship game, those who seem bored, and couples who are fighting. And you will surely notice the ones who seem happy. Which would you be?

If you and your partner were interviewed as one of those couples and compared with the others, you would likely find that the difference between you as a happy couple and you as an unhappy couple boils down to three things:

1) Taking responsibility for what you want;
2) Being clear about what you want, and;
3) Taking action toward what you want.

It's the same when applied to your sex life. The difference between you having a "regular" sex life and having a radical sex life boils down to 1) Taking responsibility for what you want, 2) Being clear about what you want, and 3) Taking action toward what you want.

So let's get back to our original questions: What kind of sexual relationship do you want? What would make you radically, ecstatically happy with your sex life beyond your wildest dreams?

Please take a moment to think about your answers. You may even want to take a break from reading for a while and write out your answers so that when we cover our sex strategies, you'll know how to apply them. But before we get into the strategies, let's look at some important research findings about sex in relationships.

Important Research Findings about Sex

*You don't have to be in the mood to become aroused
and have a satisfying orgasm.*

1. A study published in 2012 in the American Journal of Medicine studied sexual satisfaction across different age groups and found that while desire and frequency decline with age, arousal and orgasm get better. Not only does this confirm that *sex gets better with age*, it means that *desire and arousal are NOT correlated*. In other words, you don't have to be in the mood to become aroused and have a satisfying orgasm. There's also evidence out there to suggest that *having sex increases interest in sex*. The more you do it, the more you want to do it.

2. In 2010, a study published in the Archives of Sexual Behavior found that sexual satisfaction is not determined by the number of orgasms. It showed that both men and women were more satisfied when having sex out of love and commitment rather than just satisfying sexual urges. So, while recreational sex for physical pleasure might be fun, data shows that the emotional connection in a loving and committed relationship is more fulfilling.

When you are having sex as often as you like,
you are happy with your sex life.

---

3. A study published in the Journal of Sexual Marital Therapy in 2011 reported that desired frequency is a major factor in sexual satisfaction. That might seem obvious, but it's nice to have some proof that when you are having sex as often as you like, you are happy with your sex life. When you are not having sex as often as you like, you are not happy with your sex life.

Also, it should come as no surprise that men were more likely to desire sex more frequently, and many studies of sexual desire in a relationship find that, in a long-term relationship, men's desire tends to stay constant, while women's desire tends to decrease. This dynamic is a setup for relationship unhappiness and an important reason to be intentional and work together to co-create a sexual relationship that meets both partner's needs.

4. Sadly, about 20% of relationships are sexless (defined as not having sex in six weeks or more), 15% of married couples haven't had sex in six months or more, and 25% of men and women suffer from hypo-active sexual desire (HSD) and lack any interest in sex. But here's the question: Do you think couples *want* to have no interest in sex? Even if there are medical problems causing HSD, if you have low or no sexual desire but want to do something about it, you and your partner can greatly benefit from the information in this chapter.

The Benefits of Sex

Sex is not only great for a relationship; it's also great for your health. Sex lowers your stress and your blood pressure, boosts immunity, burns calories, and strengthens your heart. It releases wonderful feel-good chemicals in your body, helps you sleep better and feel better.

In the pages that follow, we'll show you exactly how to practice radical sex and live beyond happily ever after, in bed. We strongly suggest reviewing these strategies with your partner and stopping when needed to take notes and discuss the ideas we're about to share with you. A powerful practice, *Radical Sex* can transform your life and your relationship, and we want you to get full benefit by sharing and applying what you learn with your partner.

Requirements for Radical Sex

Armed with your answers to our previous questions—What kind of sexual relationship do you want? What will make you happy and satisfied with your sex life? What would make you ecstatically, radically happy beyond your wildest dreams? It's important to know what is required from you and your partner as you get into action. *Radical Sex* requires 1) radical attitude, 2) radical action, and 3) radical strategies.

Radical Sex Attitude

You strive to be the best partner you can be and co-create the sexual relationship that you both want.

Radical Sex Action

---

*You take initiative and responsibility
by doing things with and for your partner every day*

You take initiative and responsibility by doing things with and for your partner every day that benefit your sexual relationship.

Radical Sex Strategies

The achievement of any goal requires proven strategies. And radical sex requires a radical strategy. We've identified 7 *strategies for Radical Sex*, which we will examine a bit later, but first, let's lay the foundation with 7 *strategies for good, "regular" sex*.

Seven Strategies for Good Sex

Good Sex Strategy #1: Connection Rituals

---

*Rituals can be created together
to enhance your relationship.*

As mentioned in Chapter Seven, a ritual is anything you do together in your relationship on a regular basis where you generally know what it is, when it's going to happen, and where it will take place. It becomes so habitual and customary that you almost don't even need to talk about it. Many rituals evolve by themselves without intentional planning, but rituals can be created together to enhance your relationship. They are built-in ways that you can better connect with each other, every day, and you can continually refine and tweak them over time in your relationship to best suit your wants, needs, and desires.

Radical Action:

If you don't already have one, design with your partner a daily ritual for checking in with each other about your day, and include an appreciation and a request. For example-
What I most appreciate about you today is…
What would make me happy today is…

Good Sex Strategy #2: Preparation

In preparation for a good sexual experience you must first clear your mental space and be in the moment. You don't want to be fighting your mental to-do list all the while you're supposed to be connecting with your partner. You don't want to be thinking about other things or be someplace else in your head. Connection only occurs in the present. Rely on whatever strategy works best for you to be present, which might even mean taking care of some important things before you get started. And if it helps to turn off your cell phone, lock the doors, and send the kids to the movies to relax and clear your mental space, then so be it. Do whatever you need to do to make it happen.

Grooming is another thing you need to do in preparation for good sex. This may seem obvious, but sex doesn't happen with just one sense; it happens with all of them. You must take care of anything that might disagree with your partner's sense of sight, smell and taste. Make sure the whole experience turns your partner on, not off.

The setting, also, is important. By this we mean preparing the room, the bed, and the temperature—having everything ready. It's hard to do all this when it's spontaneous and spur of the moment, although that can be fun, too. But in a long-term relationship, most of the time, we get more enjoyment from our sex life when we do our best to prepare and maximize the experience.

Preparation includes comfort and privacy and making sure that you have whatever you may need to fulfill your sexual vision. That might mean lubes, sex toys, birth control, and anything you might use to enhance your sex life.

If we don't have a creative idea ahead of time,
chances are that in the moment we will end up doing
the same things we have always done.

Lastly, you might like to come prepared with creative ideas. As human beings we tend to be creatures of habit. So, if we don't have a creative idea ahead of time, chances are that in the moment we will end up doing the same things we have always done. Have fun thinking of creative ideas beforehand, and fantasize and imagine about how that's going to play out in your next sexual experience with your partner.

Radical Action:

If you don't already have one, design a shared ritual for preparing for sex. Who would do what? Where and how? What do you want your partner to do to prepare for sex? What does your partner want you to do to prepare?

Good Sex Strategy #3: Prioritizing your Partner's Fulfillment

---

You must place more emphasis
on your partner's fulfillment than your own.

If you are ever to have a truly wonderful sex life, you must place more emphasis on your partner's fulfillment than your own. We're not saying you have to neglect your own needs; we're talking a 60-40 split or so. Prioritizing your partner's fulfillment doesn't mean to devalue your own needs. It merely demonstrates the value you place on your partner's happiness in building your relationship together. It also means that your partner will do the same for you, and it becomes this sort of dance—you focus on your partner and your partner focuses on you. As a result, you both experience a sense of teamwork and shared investment in each other's fulfillment that is far greater than you could experience if you only focus on your own needs.

Imagine how good it would feel to your partner to have you prioritize his or her fulfillment. Now imagine how good it would feel if your partner prioritized your fulfillment. Your partner must be able to count on you for his or her pleasure and safety, and you must be able to count on your partner for yours.

Prioritizing your partner's fulfillment, even if it's just a little bit more than your own, makes you less self-centered, which, in any relationship, is the better position. It's not very attractive and it doesn't work very well if you are just concerned with yourself and your own pleasure. So, prioritize your partner's fulfillment, sixty percent or more. If they do the same, you will both have a great sexual relationship.

You can't be happy all by yourself,
and you can't be happy if your partner is not happy.

Mutuality in a relationship is the concept that your happiness is interdependent. You realize that you can't be happy all by yourself, and you can't be happy if your partner is not happy. Your happiness directly corresponds to your partner's happiness, which, in and of itself, is a good argument for prioritizing their happiness. Carrying out their wishes and sharing in their experience helps you both be happy.

Radical Action:

Develop the habit of checking in with your partner- "How was that for you?", "What would you like me to do?", "What would be pleasurable for you right now?"

Good Sex Strategy #4: Take Responsibility for your Fulfillment

If you are to reach your desired level of fulfillment you must practice conscious intention, which is the opposite of being passive.

When you're passive, you just let things happen. You go with the flow and you are carried with the wind. When you practice conscious intention, however, you choose what you want. You choose what kind of relationship you want, what kind of experience you want, and what kind of sex life you want—and you do something about it. You take responsibility for your own fulfillment.

It's a good thing to help your partner satisfy you.

With regard to having a good sex life, you ask for what you want and need, and then give direction to your partner to help you get it. As we discussed in Radical Communication, sometimes you might unconsciously expect your partner to read their mind, but it generally works better if you give your partner a roadmap and offer check points along the journey to keep them on course. It's a good thing to help your partner satisfy you. It's not a matter of being critical—"Oh, you're not doing it right"—although sometimes people can get defensive.

You must develop the kind of relationship where it's safe for you and your partner to ask each other for what each wants and to give directions in getting it, which we have covered in *Radical Intimacy* and *Radical Communication*.

You must remember that in a Radical Marriage, your partner actually wants to please you. Your partner doesn't want to continue doing something that really isn't working for you. In that respect, you should provide lots of direction and make lots of requests as well as welcome feedback about what would please your partner.

It's also important to practice self-management. This refers to taking care of yourself and honoring your thoughts and feelings. The idea is to commit to your experience and your connection with your partner. Again, if you're thinking about something else, you won't have a good sexual experience. You won't feel connected to your partner. Whatever experience and connection you want to have with your partner—emotional, spiritual or physical—you need to focus on that and be part of making it happen.

Radical Action:

Develop the habit of checking in with yourself by asking yourself- *What do I want? What would make me happy? What would make me feel good?* Verbalize your desires to your partner and guide them in meeting them in ways that work for you.

Good Sex Strategy #5: Structure Sex into Your Routine

Structuring sex into your routine is what we refer to as "appointment sex."

Having a certain time and day when you know it's going to happen allows for planning and creativity.

If you know when you will have sex, then you can look forward to it and fantasize about what's coming. It builds anticipation. Still, this doesn't mean that you have to wait for your appointment. The seduction and foreplay can start hours before. Having a certain time and day when you know it's going to happen allows for planning and creativity as we already mentioned. You can be much more creative planning in advance than on the spur of the moment. And just to be clear, appointment sex doesn't need to replace spontaneous sex. You can do both!

Sex dates promote security. You don't have to wonder *When is the next time we're going to have sex?* You and your partner can both mentally, physically, and emotionally prepare and feel comfortable knowing exactly when you will next have sex. Thinking about sex by planning your next session actually counters diminishing desire, a natural occurrence that happens with long-term relationships, especially as we age.

Having sex, as we now know, increases interest in sex. It's very much like exercise. If you don't exercise, you don't feel motivated to exercise. If you exercise regularly it becomes a habit, you enjoy it, and you miss it when you don't have it. It's the same for sex. The more you do it, the more you want to do it, and the better your life and relationship will be.

Radical Action:

Discuss with your partner your preferred times and days for scheduled sex and develop a plan to structure sex into your routine in a way that works for both of you.

Good Sex Strategy #6: Embrace What Is

*Your attitude towards sex
determines your experience of sex.*

Sex is in your head more than in your body. Your attitude towards sex determines your experience of sex. "Embracing what is" includes things like erectile performance: If you have an erection, great. Even if you have erectile dysfunction (impotence) you can still have a great sexual experience. There are lots of men that have ED—15% of men over 40 and 25% of men over 65.

At some point every man will experience ED or the difficulty of having an erection. It doesn't have to interfere with having a fulfilling sexual experience with your partner. It will only get in the way if you let it by associating good sex with always having an erection.

In life, relationships, and sex we must embrace what *is.* Arousal comes and goes. It's high sometimes; it's low at other times. It really doesn't matter what your level of arousal is, or your partner's for that matter. If one person is ready to go and the other really isn't, that's okay. Wherever you are in that moment ... just embrace what *is.*

Many people say, "I'm not in the mood," and for them, if they're not in the mood then it's not going to happen. But as we've mentioned earlier, you can embrace not being in the mood. "Honey, I'm really not in the mood tonight, but let's hop into bed and see what happens." Trust us—and the data backs this up—it works!

*If you abstain from sex every time you're tired,
and many couples do, it means you will rarely have sex.*

Embracing what *is* also includes embracing your energy level. Sometimes you will be tired, and sometimes your partner will be tired. Often, in relationships, that is a reason for not having sex. But we disagree with that. If you abstain from sex every time you're tired, and many couples do, it means you will rarely have sex. We're all tired from time to time, but there is a way to have great sex with a low level of energy. We call it *passive sex.*

Passive Sex

Passive Sex means making the most of the energy you *do* have. Sometimes that means you're just a more passive partner, which is okay. It doesn't mean you're not connecting emotionally, or just lying there, not really participating. You are participating, but in a passive way. "Honey, I'm really tired tonight, but I'm quite happy to just lay here and let you do whatever you want to do with my body."

Embracing *what is* also includes embracing your orgasm. You embrace your experience and you don't get attached to one particular outcome. In other words, orgasm is great if it happens, but you can still have a great time together without it.

Embracing the effects of aging is another aspect of embracing what *is*. We all age and we can't get away from that. When you're young it seems like you will live forever and the way it *is* will be forever. Over time you learn the hard way that isn't the case. What came easily and worked regularly before, all of a sudden doesn't come as easily and doesn't work as regularly as it did.

Age brings change, and it will definitely affect your life. To have a fulfilling relationship and sex life you must embrace that. You must accept its perks and downsides, and you must age with grace. You must accept the new normal, which doesn't mean it's worse. It just means it's different.

Embrace what is and focus on your connection
and the experience you have with your partner,
here and now, and you will have a great relationship
and sex life—no matter what happens.

The most important part of embracing what *is*, in our opinion, is to focus on your connection with your partner. Again, we're not talking about a specific outcome; we're talking about the overall experience with your partner. If you are unable to focus on connection, you and your partner will set yourselves up for frustration and disappointment. Embrace what *is* and focus on your connection and the experience you have with your partner, here and now, and you will have a great relationship and sex life—no matter what happens.

Radical Action:

Don't let "reasons" (being tired, busy, not in the mood, etc.) interfere with appointment sex. Keep your appointment no matter what, accept what is, let go of the outcome, and focus on connecting with your partner physically, emotionally, and spiritually.

Good Sex Strategy #7: Debrief Ritual

A *debrief ritual* means that after sex, you have regular time set aside to talk about your latest sexual experience. It doesn't mean it has to be right away; it could be the next day, before you go to bed, or when you're pillow talking. The important thing is that you take time to discuss your experiences.

Reliving your sexual experiences together
is a great turn on.

As a general rule, we highly recommend *connection* rituals, and this can be one of them. The idea is to share your thoughts, feelings and experiences with your partner. It's very intimate and reliving your sexual experiences together is a great turn on. Yes, it's wonderful to have the sexual experience in the first place, but it's also fun to talk about it, and relive it again.

From personal experience we can tell you that talking about sex helps you and your partner get in the mood again. And we don't mean only talking about what you enjoyed; you must also explore what you didn't like and what you would do differently next time. This isn't criticism or saying a partner did something wrong; it's acknowledging that there will often be a gap between what you wanted and what actually happened. And the best way to close that gap is to talk about it.

One strategy you might remember from The Relationship Journal is to give your last sexual experience a rating. Rate it on a scale from 1 to 10, keeping in mind that it's not the score that is important. What's important is what's needed to make it a 10. "You know, Honey, last time we made love that was about a 7 for me and what would make it a 10 would be this, and this, and this."

The rating system identifies the gap between what actually happened and what would make you happy, excited, and fulfilled. The more you talk about it, the easier it is to close the gap. From personal experience we can tell you that you won't have to do this forever. Within a short period of time, you will better understand your partner and get more in touch with your own needs. Eventually, the rating system will become more or less obsolete, because the gap will have diminished to the point where you both are having the exact experiences that you want.

It Ain't Easy

We understand that talking about what did and didn't work during any sexual experience is difficult for a lot of people. But it gets easier over time. It will work well as long as you create a safe space for this kind of conversation where you and your partner understand that you are not criticizing, you're just working together to create a better mutual experience. And your sex life and relationship will be better for it. If talking about sex is challenging for you, The Relationship Journal can be useful by first writing down your thoughts and sharing with your partner by having them read your entry, which can then make it easier to talk about it.

Most couples don't have these kinds of intimate, sexually explicit conversations, but to have a Radical Marriage, you must talk about EVERYTHING. This includes those areas of your life where you haven't gone before. You must talk specifically and explicitly about your sex life and what you want and what you desire in this area. If you want good sex you must talk about it with your partner. If you don't, you will leave things to chance and you will not be fully satisfied with your sexual relationship.

Couples that talk explicitly about sex
are dramatically happier in their relationship.

The couples that talk explicitly about sex are dramatically happier in their relationship. They view sex as a chance to connect and communicate with their partner. It gives them an opportunity to examine what's going on for them, what they want, and what would make things better for both parties.

Radical Action:

Determine the best way to fit a debrief ritual into your routine and share what you enjoyed and what you'd like to do differently next time. Use the Relationship Journal if needed.

Now that we've laid the foundation with strategies for regular *"good"* sex, let's raise the bar and explore seven out-of-the-box, creative strategies for *Radical Sex*.

188

Seven Strategies for Radical Sex

In this section we cover seven strategies for taking your sexual relationship far beyond what most couples experience. These strategies build upon the seven *good* sex strategies we covered earlier, so if you skipped them, we recommend going back to the previous section.

Important Radical Sex Questions

So what kind of sexual relationship do you want? Daily sex? Sex whenever you want? Adventurous sex? Do you want extraordinary sex but don't know how to get your partner on board? Is there a kinky thing or two you've always wanted to try ... but didn't dare to? Is there something you've always wanted to do with your partner that you've been too embarrassed to talk about? What would make you ecstatically, radically happy beyond your wildest dreams?

Take a few moments ... think about it, talk about it, write about it ... and explore your deepest sexual desires. When you're finished, let's explore our seven strategies for *Radical Sex*.

Radical Sex Strategy #1: Identify your biggest dream or vision for your sexual relationship

---

*The simple practice of being clear about your goal
makes it possible to achieve it.*

As we mentioned earlier in this book, the simple practice of being clear about your goal makes it possible to achieve it. After all, if you don't know what you want, how can you expect to get it? All the strategies in the world won't help you if you can't apply them to a specific goal. We suggest getting started with a mini relationship retreat using The Relationship Journal, where you spend a few hours, or even a whole day, talking about what you want with your partner. Whether you get away to a romantic location or do this at home, together you can create a shared vision for your relationship and sex life that excites and motivates both of you for years to come.

Radical Action:

Schedule a mini relationship retreat with your partner TODAY.

Radical Sex Strategy #2: Practice Radical Intimacy

By now you should be well versed in the concept of *Radical Intimacy* where we stress the importance of creating emotional safety for yourself and your partner. Having an emotionally safe relationship is critical to having a great relationship and *Radical Sex*, because you must continually take emotional risks. In a sexual relationship, taking emotional risks means talking about things that you might be embarrassed to talk about or even feel a sense of shame.

We all have hang-ups and it's not easy to talk about this stuff.

We all have hang-ups and it's not easy to talk about this stuff. But when you're in a committed relationship and you know your partner isn't going anywhere, there are plenty of daily opportunities to think about things and clarify your needs. So, take a chance and go ahead and talk about them. When you do, you must tell the whole truth—and that means everything!

When you tell your truth, it will be more than just a sentence. There will be something beyond that, and underneath that, and something else after that. To be *radical*, your partner must know everything related to what is going on for you—what you want, need, and desire.

As a refresher, *Radical Intimacy* requires *positive response*, which means you never say "no." This scares some people to death. "What? Never say 'no'? Shouldn't I have boundaries?" Well, yes,

190

you should have boundaries. But you should also never shoot down your partner's request outright. Instead of saying "No," respond positively with what you CAN do.

Positive response is part of *Radical Intimacy*, which creates emotional safety. It means that partners can count on each other to not reject them, turn them down, or turn them away. Instead partners let each other know what does work for them and what they are willing to do, which fosters trust and connection.

In practicing *Radical Intimacy*, it's also important to push your upper limit. We all have a limit on how much happiness we can stand and if we want *Radical Sex* or a *Radical Marriage*, we need to push our upper limit so we can accept more happiness and more fulfillment. Believe it or not, when we reach our upper limit, it's not comfortable. As a result we often sabotage ourselves, doing what we need to do to bring things down to a more comfortable level. We must acknowledge that we have an upper limit and work to expand that limit to bring more happiness into our lives.

Radical Action:

Review the chapter on Radical Intimacy and implement the suggested strategies in your relationship. This is truly the foundation of Radical Sex.

Radical Sex Strategy #3: Share and Explore All Your Fantasies and Desires

---

*We keep secrets, and then
we become ashamed of our secrets.*

When we were kids we had a vivid imagination and we were encouraged to use it. As adults, however, we often think and fantasize about all kinds of stuff that we are embarrassed to talk about with others. We may not even want to admit our "naughty" thoughts to ourselves. We tend to live in "reality" and curb our imagination. We suppress it. We keep secrets, and then we become ashamed of our secrets.

You need to give permission to yourself and your partner to have fantasies and desires. As an adult in a safe, committed relationship, it's okay to finally share your deepest secrets. You can explore any and all fantasies and desires with your partner. This doesn't mean you'll actually get to do all of them, but you can still share them.

You might have a fantasy of jumping off a cliff without a parachute … or having sex with 50 partners in one night. That may understandably be a fantasy your partner doesn't share. But that shouldn't stop you from sharing all of your fantasies and desires with your partner, because in a Radical Marriage your partner should not judge you as being wrong for having them.

With regard to *Radical Sex*, you know who your partner is and you accept that they have fantasies, and, even if you don't go along with them exactly, you should at least try to respond with something that would be okay to do around that fantasy.

We must give ourselves permission
to let our energy go where it wants to go.

When you are sharing and exploring all of your fantasies and desires, you must be unencumbered and go where your energy wants to go. We all have passions, interests, desires, and likes. We feel free and happy, contented and fulfilled when we are able to fully be who we are and express our truth. If we suppress our truth we can feel frustrated and disappointed and even depressed. We must give ourselves permission to let our energy go where it wants to go.

If our energy carries us into an area that is taboo, or leads us to something that is not realistic, like having sex with 50 different partners in one night, we can still find creative ways to make it acceptable and doable. It's fun and exciting to embrace each other's fantasies and desires and be creative and experimental in exploring them together.

Radical Sex involves taking the risk of sharing your fantasies and desires with your partner. Yes, it might feel scary. But it is also exciting when you do it, especially if you receive a positive response. Who knows? Your partner might share your fantasy, whatever it is. "Ooh, that's exciting! Let's try that!" Or your partner might not be as enthused about it, but still be willing to try it, for you. "Well, I'm not really into that, but I'd be willing to support you in that fantasy, so, let's experiment."

Radical Action:

Develop the habit of sharing with your partner, in real time as it happens, when you have a fantasy or desire, about sex or anything else. Sharing these thoughts that you would typically keep to yourself can feel risky, but will deepen your intimacy, connection, and adventurousness in your relationship.

Radical Sex Strategy #4: Daily Sex

Having daily sex simply means that you build it into your routine. Remember earlier when we talked about not being attached to a particular outcome? Here, you have an appointment to have sex, follow through on your commitment, and it is what it is. It does not have to be five hours long; it doesn't even have to be an hour long and it doesn't even need to result in climax. It could be a quick thing as you get in bed before you go to sleep, or in the morning as a pleasurable way to start the day, or on the couch during commercials while watching TV, or in the bath or shower. Whatever it is, it's built into your routine. But it's also optional. You can always put it off. You can always say, "You know what? How about we skip it today?"

193

As long as you keep your appointment most days, then skipping it once in a great while is not a big deal. If you have sex once a week or longer and you skip it, and the next time you have sex is going to be another week or month, then skipping it *is* a big deal.

Daily sex gives you a lot of comfort and security, as well as a lot of great sexual experiences. It also makes it much easier to put it off when the timing isn't right. So build it in your routine. You can even put it on the calendar (in code!) where it serves as a daily reminder that you prioritize your relationship and that you look forward to intimate contact, every day.

Private Touching

Private touching means that you touch your partner and your partner touches you in a way that nobody else touches you and nobody else touches your partner.

Private touching is another aspect of daily sex. Private touching means that you touch your partner and your partner touches you in a way that nobody else touches you and nobody else touches your partner. It's intimate and private between the two of you.

Let's say a couple is watching TV and the husband fondles his wife's breast. That's an example of private touching. The husband wouldn't just fondle any woman; he only does so with his wife. You can take private touching as far as you want to take it, and you can do it on a daily basis, which would be "daily sex."

Remember, we all have boundaries, and we assert those boundaries with people that we don't know. We don't let anybody touch us in ways that we don't want to be touched. But we lower those boundaries with our partner and we want them to touch us. It feels good when they touch us, and it feels good when we touch them.

Ideally, private touching is something you would talk about; you wouldn't necessarily just do it. It wouldn't feel so good if you tried private touching and your partner just moved your hand away, saying "Stop it, that doesn't feel good." Private touching is not about leading up to anything. It's not suggesting intercourse. It's not even foreplay. It's just a fun, pleasurable, connecting activity all by itself.

The fun part of private touching is that
you can do it almost anywhere and anytime,
as long as it is private and it is fun all by itself.

So, daily sex will sometimes mean the full-blown routine—intercourse and orgasm—but not always. Sometimes it means subtle and private connection, the low-key stuff like private touching. The fun part of private touching is that you can do it almost anywhere and anytime, as long as it is private and it is fun all by itself. It expresses attraction. It says "I am attracted to you. I want to be with you." It also expresses appreciation. "I appreciate you as my partner. I appreciate you as my sexual partner. I appreciate the things you do for me. I want to be with you, I want to touch you and I want to be touched by you."

Daily sex definitely requires a *radical relationship*. So if you're having difficulty with the idea or the implementation of it, please re-read the previous chapters, as they set the stage for this phase of the marriage.

Radical Action:

Get started with Daily Sex by initiating a daily routine of private touching. Talk with each other about the possibilities and what forms of private touching would be OK and welcomed. Radical Sex is about expanding your experiences and practices beyond your everyday routine and comfort level, so do your best to lower your boundaries and try things you normally would not.

195

Radical Sex Strategy #5: Expand Beyond Traditional Intercourse

When most people think sex they think intercourse. However, if you're practicing *Radical Sex* then traditional intercourse becomes boring, and as we've discussed earlier, it becomes almost impossible to do every day, especially as you age. Life gets exciting when you begin to expand beyond traditional intercourse. Yes, you *can* have intercourse every day, but it's good to explore what else you can do.

You can be creative and adventurous and you can push the envelope and try different things. Trying different things may even lead to you finding your new favorite thing. Then you can do that again and find another favorite thing. Before you know it, your sexual repertoire will be greatly increased beyond traditional intercourse.

There are many more sexually adventurous alternatives to explore than you can possibly do in a lifetime.

There are many more sexually adventurous alternatives to explore than you can possibly do in a lifetime, such as erotic massage, Tantra, fetishes, toys, and mutual masturbation. You can even explore erotic videos and porn—which are not the same thing—and there is even a category for female-friendly porn.

---

*Instead of doing things in secret,
separate from your partner, do them with your partner.*

It's also worth noting that masturbation and porn are often solo activities. A person might watch porn alone and wouldn't dream about doing that with a partner. Or a person might masturbate and keep that a secret, too. In *Radical Sex*, we highly recommend taking some of the things that you might be ashamed of, embarrassed about, or do in private, and share them with your partner. This is a Radical Marriage, where your intimacy and sexual relationship grows. Instead of doing things in secret, separate from your partner, do them with your partner. We promise that it's fun and fulfilling.

You might also try erotic talk or reading erotic books together. Ever heard of 50 *Shades of Grey?* It comes as a trilogy and should keep you busy for a while. You might also try erotic games. There are even erotic apps for your smart phone. Sex furniture and mirrors are fun. Role-playing is also an option. Or, how about a sex swing?

Sex swings deserve a special shout out from our list of the many things you can do to create fulfilling and new sexual experiences, because not only are they a lot of fun, they also come in handy when one partner has physical limitations. Yes, sex swings make sex more exciting and easy, as they allow for greater freedom of movement during intercourse and offer unique sexual positions. But they also help individuals with muscular weakness or arthritis, who can use sex swings to enjoy sexual activity without straining weak muscles or painful joints. If you have trouble finding a comfortable sex swing in your area you can try www.bit.ly/passion-swing. Sex swings can be used with a stand or hung from the ceiling or a doorway.

(And here's a trick for hiding the evidence in the ceiling to prevent curious questions from your kids or friends: *Just take the guts out of the smoke detector, place it over the eyebolt, and no one will know the difference. Shh...*)

Radical Action:

Brainstorm and research alternatives together (you can use the above ideas as a start) and try one new "non-traditional" form of sex once a month or so, and have fun!

Radical Sex Strategy #6: Learn

Learning new things helps expand your possibilities.

Learning new things helps expand your possibilities in any relationship, especially when it comes to your sex life. You might think you know all there is to know about sex and relationships, but one of our favorite sayings is "You don't know what you don't know!" Even after decades living and breathing relationships as a profession, we continue to discover and learn new things about ourselves, our relationship, and sex, which makes our life together a true adventure.

How do you find new things to learn? Well, you can learn by doing, but you can also look for outside help. There are lots of books and instructional videos that are fun to check out together. There are workshops and classes, and you can even hire a sex coach. You can try new practices, and you can find ideas for these new practices on the Internet. For example, you may have heard of Tantra, but there is another approach that we recently discovered called Orgasmic Meditation (OM), a 15-minute ritual that can make a huge difference in your sex life.

Regarding OM, many women want their partners to slow down and many men would like to but don't really know how. So guys, if you like the idea of being able to provide your woman a 15-minute orgasm, get the book *Slow Sex* by Nicole Daedone and watch the Orgasmic Meditation videos at onetaste.us. And gals, if you want more emotional and spiritual connection with your partner, if you seek a totally and relaxing and pleasurable way to become aroused and experience bliss even if you're not in the mood, or if you've given up hope in ever experiencing an orgasm, Orgasmic Meditation is for you and definitely qualifies as a recommended Radical Sex strategy in our opinion.

Radical Action:

Surf the internet, Amazon, and elsewhere to find books, videos, websites, etc., select a few gems to share with your partner, and have fun exploring new territory together!

Radical Sex Strategy #7: Compile Your Radical Sex Playlist

Just like a playlist of your favorite songs on your iPod, your *Radical Sex playlist* is a selection of your favorite sexual routines. More than specific activities like a certain sexual position, these routines are more like a favorite dance or ritual that you want to experience regularly. Mix them with other favorite routines and you get even more enjoyable variety.

One of your goals in being adventurous and finding your new favorite thing is to add to your *Radical Sex playlist*. Some examples might include Toy Day, Role-Play Day, Swing Day, Erotic Massage Day, Romantic Bath Day, Pleasure-Him Day, Pleasure-Her Day. Or how about Orgasmic Meditation Day, Erotic Book Day, or Erotic Video Day?

It's fun to plan ahead together and prepare and anticipate what's going to happen when the time comes.

This strategy works well when combined with appointment sex as it's fun to plan ahead together and prepare and anticipate what's going to happen when the time comes.

Whatever you decide, we sincerely hope that you find our suggestions helpful and that you have some solid ideas planned to incorporate *Radical Sex* into your *Radical Marriage*. But please do remember that talking to your partner about *Radical Sex* has consequences. It's the only way to have a fulfilling relationship, but not all relationships can handle honest discussion about these things. If this is your situation, please get the support you need from a qualified therapist, counselor, or coach.

Your relationship is worth a little extra effort and help. No one is successful alone and a little bit of support can go a long way in implementing Radical Sex strategies for taking your relationship beyond happily ever. Speaking of which, let's tie it all together as we send you on your way with our next and final chapter, *Radical Living*.

Summary of Good Sex Strategies

1. Connection rituals
2. Preparation
3. Prioritizing your partner's fulfillment
4. Take responsibility for your fulfillment
5. Structure sex into your routine
6. Embrace "what is"
7. Debrief ritual

Summary of Radical Sex Strategies

1. Identify your biggest dream or vision for your sexual relationship
2. Practice Radical Intimacy
3. Share and explore all your fantasies and desires
4. Daily sex
5. Expand beyond traditional intercourse
6. Learn
7. Compile your Radical Sex playlist

Chapter Ten: Radical Living

As you blend the lessons of each of the chapters in this book, you will notice that each of the areas are like puzzle pieces that come together to comprise a Radical Marriage. Like a team or partners in a relationship, each makes the other stronger and capable of more. Combining each element helps you improve upon not only your relationship together, but every aspect of your existence as you look ahead to *Radical Living*.

---

*We must accept that life is always changing
and we will not be around forever.*

We have a natural tendency to reflect back on our lives, and in moderation this can be a meaningful exercise. But we must live in the present and do our best to appreciate every moment going forward. We must accept that life is always changing and we will not be around forever. We must focus on making the biggest difference we can so that every day of our life we are maximizing our contribution to our work, our lives, and our families.

What is Radical Living?

As human beings we have a desire and the need for comfort. We have a comfort level. We have a pain threshold, a level below which things are uncomfortable and painful. We also have an upper limit. Very few people know or understand this, but we can only handle so much happiness. We have an upper limit that prevents us from being too happy. Our job in life is to push that upper limit, so that we can handle more happiness in our life.

*You cannot be happy and successful and fulfilled
living within your comfort level.*

Radical Living is about living on the edge and about going for it and about allowing yourself to be increasingly happy and accomplished with respect to whatever your dreams are so that we are raising that upper limit. The key is to go beyond your comfort level. You cannot live a radical life, you cannot be happy and successful and fulfilled living within your comfort level. You must break through and fully live the adventure that is life.

So, what is your biggest dream for your life? What do you want that you are aware of and can conceive right now? What would you be ecstatic about that you aren't even aware of yet? How can you keep your life fresh and exciting and continually evolving? How can you live life to the fullest, with your partner, with the time you have left on this planet?

It starts with vision.

Vision

As we have stressed throughout the book, you must first be aware that there is *more* there. Then you must get in touch with what that is. Some of it you won't discover until you get there, because you won't be able to fully see everything until you start accomplishing some of your dreams and desires. Other things you can absolutely uncover right now.

There's a wonderful aspect of coaching that we call visioning. It consists of helping you get in touch with what you really want, and going beyond that. It's helping you uncover things that you want, need, and desire—perhaps some things you weren't even aware of, and some things you were aware of years ago and forgot about.

You do have a purpose in life. You have a desire for significance. You want your life to mean something. You want to leave behind a legacy of some kind. What is it? First you must define it in the form of a vision. Living it out is part of what we call *Radical Living*.

When you are on track with what you were meant to do, you will shine, blossom, and accomplish great things. If you are off track with your life purpose, you become depressed, discouraged, or frustrated. You may not even know why or how to fix it. And that's one of the greatest contributions of the field of professional coaching: helping you discover and live your life purpose.

You must first be able to see what you want from your life and your relationship in order to get it.

Remember, "what you believe and conceive, you can achieve," and by extension, what you don't believe and can't conceive, you can't achieve. We are not saying it is easy and there are many reasons for "no." There are countless obstacles to the many things that you might want, but you must first be able to see what you want from your life and your relationship in order to get it.

Vision is crucial for happiness and fulfillment. Vision is grand. Vision is energy. The clearer you are about your vision, the easier it is to make it happen. Vision helps us recognize the available opportunities and resources to get what we really want. It's inside us and it guides us. It steers us toward certain choices and away from others.

If you have ever wondered if you have a vision, all you have to do is pay attention when you are faced with making a choice. A reaction like *This feels good* or *This doesn't feel good* or *I'm not so sure about this* is your vision guiding you. It's not always your head evaluating the variables, it's your intuition. It has to *feel* right. It has to fit what's on the inside trying to express itself on the outside.

Yes, Yes, Hell No

A friend of ours, Brian Whetten, has written a book called *Yes Yes Hell No*. In his book, Brian proposes that we have three parts of ourselves—mind, spirit, and body. Our *mind* is our cognition, reasoning, and logic. Our *spirit* is our intuition or inner voice. Our *body* is where we find our basic, instinctive, reactive *emotions*, especially fear.

Brian asserts that when we are making decisions or taking action, sometimes our intuition will tell us "Yes, this is a good decision," and our head will tell us "Go for it," however, because it pushes our comfort level and we experience a bit of fear, our emotions come in and say "Hell No!"

How do you know if your fear is helping you survive or holding you back?

As human beings we are conditioned to listen to our fear. It's how we survive. But how do you know if your fear is helping you survive or holding you back?

According to Brian, based on years of mistakes, experience, and success, if your intuition and your brain line up, even if you feel fear, then you should feel the fear and do it anyway. *Yes, Yes, Hell No* means *do it*. But if you feel fear and your head says this is too much of a risk, or your gut says this is not a good idea, then don't do it.

Whetten's strategy can help you make decisions along the way, but again, you must first have a vision to know where you want to go in the first place.

According to Gottman

Dr. John Gottman, the premiere researcher studying relationships and marriage, has written several seminal books in the field. He has also uncovered some interesting data about the role of vision. Gottman's research shows that 69% of conflict in couple relationships is due to "unrealized expectations" for their life and relationship together. Analyzing this research and interpreting the words, we see that "unrealized expectations" is another way of representing what we call *vision*. Put simply, your vision is what you want to realize. It is what you expect and what you go after in your life and relationship.

Gottman also explains his findings in terms of dreams, stating that conflict often happens when you have a dream for your life or for your relationship that either isn't being realized or isn't being supported by your partner. Tragically, most couples are not even aware of the root of their problem, and the conflict goes on and on, unresolved.

We all want happiness and fulfillment. That's what drives us into a relationship in the first place. It's our vision that helps us reach our wildest dreams, and in the case of *Radical Living*, beyond them. But it's not enough to explore the important elements of vision, we must also examine how to achieve it and what gets in the way.

Relationship Skills

Even though relationship skills are an important part of life, they are given little if any attention in school. Degree programs focus on how to tackle the technical aspects of a career but not how to relate to others. And yet, relationships are at the foundation of whether we are happy and achieve our vision.

Part of the problem is immature attitudes—for instance, not being able to manage our own emotional reactivity and our own role in any particular conflict. There is also an inability to negotiate differences stemming from ineffective communication skills.

Immature relationship attitudes
translate to ineffective communication.

Commonly, immature relationship attitudes translate to ineffective communication when you listen for as long as someone agrees with you. When they stop agreeing with you, you stop listening. All the while you are already formulating in your own mind what you are going to say back to the other person as they are talking— sometimes you don't even let them finish before you interject your thoughts. That's not effective listening. Also, as we have discussed elsewhere in this book, it's ineffective to have opinions, judgments and interpretations and impose them on others as truth or facts. It's a common thing we do, and it's highly ineffective.

Conflict = Opportunity

Regardless of the tack you take, if you are to enjoy *Radical Living* you must avoid playing it too safe. One way to do that is to view relationship conflict as an opportunity. You might also call it growth.

There really is hidden treasure in any conflict.

Couples often get stuck in quicksand in their communication, sinking deeper and deeper into the abyss. They are unable to see where the gold is, because they think the conflict or the partner is the problem. But there really is hidden treasure in any conflict. Couples just have to focus on where to find it.

We all have unconscious stuff going on. We have different motivations in our interactions with people. Sometimes we feel safe enough to approach someone with positive energy. Sometimes we avoid relationships altogether, and we direct our energy somewhere else. Sometimes we attack people with negative energy and don't even know why we do it. We remain unconscious about what's really going on inside; therefore, we're not really able to manage our reactivity. This sabotages our ability to fulfill our vision, and what gets in the way is more a matter of *functioning*.

Two Aspects of Functioning

Relationships are a learning laboratory
for us to learn how to accept and negotiate our differences.

There are two aspects of functioning in a relationship. One is your *attitude* and the other is your *skillset*. Each manifests in areas with concrete differences, which, by the way, are not necessarily bad. Everyone is different. We *should* be different. No matter how well traveled or enlightened you may be, it's impossible to find somebody exactly like you. Search far and wide and you still won't find anybody that will agree with everything you say and do. There's a reason for that—relationships are a learning laboratory for us to learn how to accept and negotiate our differences. It's a critical skill to function in life and love.

Recognizing Sources of Conflict and Challenge

Money

With all the differences that creep into our relationships, you would be hard-pressed to find a more common source of problems than money. When it comes to money, people are unique in how they handle it, spend it, save it, budget it, and earn it. Not surprisingly, it makes it one of the top areas of conflict in relationships.

Despite all the controversy it can bring, money is critical to achieving your vision. It's impossible to be fulfilled without a certain amount of money in your life, that is, unless you want to be a monk or live "off the grid." For the rest of us, money is crucial to achieving happiness, and couples must work as a team to get on the same page about it.

Being on the same page doesn't mean agreeing. It doesn't mean thinking exactly the same way. It means understanding where you and your partner are coming from and figuring out how to move forward together. You don't have to have the same reasons for what you do and you don't have to do it the same way. It's okay, even expected, that you and your partner will see and do things differently. In fact, a lot of the fun in a relationship is seeing how creative you can get in implementing a solution that fits you both. But if you are ever to enjoy Radical Living, you must eventually work together in achieving your goals, a topic that we will explore in more detail a bit later.

Domestic Issues

Domestic issues are another big source of conflict and challenge in a relationship. These are things like chores, neatness, organization, decorating, and home improvements. When it comes to these items, it's common for folks to avoid conflict altogether by going along: "Okay, we'll do it your way. Whatever you want, Dear."

The problem is when you do this too much, you end up resenting it, and it leaks out in other ways. It comes out in different areas, for instance digging in and fighting tooth and nail over the restaurant that you want to go to, because you're so tired of never doing what *you* want.

When people are in a relationship they must honor
what the other person wants as well as their own preferences.

In a relationship, both people must take care of themselves. They must both assert themselves. When people are in a relationship they must honor what the other person wants as well as their own preferences. When they do that they will find a way, most of the time, to make each other happy and reach a heightened state of fulfillment.

Getting back to John Gottman, his research shows that most men think they're doing more than they really are—Gottman not excluded. He says he must ask his wife to make sure that he is carrying his share of the load, because he often thinks that he is, even when he isn't. Gottman also says that women interpret doing chores around the house as a sign of love. As a result, women feel more sexually responsive when their husband is doing his part. Turns out, doing chores is an amazing aphrodisiac! This is a good thing for guys to know, and a good thing for women to tell them, if they don't know it already. Pass it on.

Family

Another common challenge in relationships has to do with extended family—the in-laws. No one has the perfect family. However, we're much more desensitized to *our* family than our *partner's* family. Things we might accept easily and take for granted with our own family might really bug our partner. And vice-versa. This leads to potential problems.

Let's take for example the question of how we spend holidays. This is often a huge challenge, because both families probably have different ways of doing things. As couples, we must figure out how to accommodate the rituals of others and if we plan to develop rituals of our own, which can be a real challenge. In fact, figuring out how to handle holidays is probably the biggest developmental step for a new couple. We can't please everyone and we can't be everywhere on Thanksgiving. We can try, but we are facing an uphill battle. For a relationship to work, couples must reach a level of maturity and really know how to communicate with each other.

Gender Differences

There is so much that can go wrong in a relationship and so many possible areas of conflict that can cause problems. One of them is gender differences. We were taught that there are very few scientifically provable gender differences; however, there are some that are culturally socialized. But we do have differences that show up along gender lines, even if we don't call them gender differences.

It is common for women to want to talk and experience connection with their partner before becoming sexual. It is common for men to become sexually aroused easily and not need any connection time prior to sexual activity. After orgasm, however, men become more cuddly, communicative, and connection-oriented. This is a clear, easy-to-see gender difference.

Other areas of disparity include sexual desire and style. For example, it's common for partners to not want sex at exactly the same time all the time in exactly the same way. We must recognize this and respect it. We must be kind to each other in that sense. We can develop rituals that encourage each other to participate and become close. Both partners must hone the ability to initiate sex and connection, and not fall into a rut of one person always being the initiator and one person always being more passive about it.

Men feel most connected and good about themselves and the relationship when they feel that they are protective and competent. Men prefer to feel "in charge" and "in control." They like to know that everything and everyone is safe—the doors and windows are locked and the baseball bat is by the bed. Men like to feel capable of protecting their family from outside threats.

Women have a little different style. Sure, they can be protective, especially when it comes to their children, but women often express themselves in a way that, unfortunately, from the men's perspective, comes out as a complaint. It may be simply something that's wrong or something that they want changed, but men hear it differently. Men hear a complaint and it makes them feel like they are not doing their job. It feels bad, like they are inadequate or there is something wrong with them. After all, if men had been doing their job, women wouldn't be complaining about it—or so it seems. Similarly, women are often made to feel as if they are always complaining when in fact they may be just expressing their point of view.

Men and women connect differently. Women don't necessarily need you to "fix it". If you're a guy, how many times have you heard this? "I'm not asking you to solve it. I just need you to listen." Underneath the universal "complaint" of women is their longing to connect to men— and a fear that they're not going to be able to do it. We must all learn to understand our gender differences and communicate more effectively to get on with Radical Living.

As a refresher from radical communication on how to do this, women can simply turn a perceived complaint into a request so the guy knows what to do. "Oh! You want me to do this? I can do that!" This subtle change becomes more effective, and addresses one of the more interesting gender differences.

Adaptations

Adaptations occur when you take on a role,
make a choice, or perform a behavior,
without really thinking or talking about it.

Another common relationship challenge that gets in the way of realizing a vision has to do with what we call *adaptations*. Adaptations occur when you take on a role, make a choice, or perform a behavior, without really thinking or talking about it; you just adapt to the situation.

Some adaptations are functional, like household chores. For instance, your partner may never take out the garbage. Why should they? They know you'll do it. It wasn't always that way, but you have consistently taken the initiative and your partner has adapted. After a while, though, you might think, *Hey, why am I the only one who ever takes out the garbage around here?* Mundane tasks such as this often lead to marital conflict.

In relationships we adapt to each other in many ways—a lot of them unconscious. We described another version of this earlier in the book when talking about compromising on movies. Often adaptations create conflict when our styles of adapting either no longer work or eventually come to a head.

Kids and Parenting

Typically, when you envision your ideal marriage, arguing about how to handle the kids is not part of it. The truth is, parenting is another big area of challenge in a relationship. So, if you have kids in the picture there is no question that you and your partner will differ in your approach to raising them. You will differ on how to handle them, how to discipline them, how to feed them, and how to take care of them.

We care about our kids. They are important to us. We want to be good parents. We want to do it right. It's no wonder that we have strong opinions about what is best for our kids. And we often have different ideas about what that means. In fact, Gottman points out that after the birth of a child, marital satisfaction goes down significantly.

Welcoming a baby into a couple's life is a time of huge transition and it's difficult to manage. Just knowing that it's normal can help you avoid getting so bent out of shape about it. Sadly, many divorces occur after children have come into the picture. Couples that once had manageable relationships often can't find a way to work together with kids, which is no fault of the children.

Emotional Needs

Last on our list of common challenges in a relationship that interfere with achieving a vision has to do with different ways that we feel loved. We call these emotional needs. Two of the most important kinds of needs in a relationship are *functional needs* and *emotional need*s. *Functional needs* include chores, money, and other necessities of life in a civilized culture. *Emotional needs,* which we will now discuss, revolve around how we feel loved, and they are different for everybody.

The Platinum Rule

*Things that make us feel loved are not necessarily
those that make our partner feel loved.*

The best way to help a person feel loved is to practice what we call the Platinum Rule. If you don't know what that is, it may help to compare it to the Golden Rule. The Golden Rule, often cited, is *do unto others as you would have them do unto you*. This is a good rule as it's helpful for living in a civilized society where people treat others as they would want to be treated, and don't do to others what they wouldn't want. But it's not without its shortcomings. In a relationship, because we want to feel loved and because we are different, the things that make us feel loved are not necessarily those that make our partner feel loved. To remedy this we recommend the Platinum Rule, which is, *do unto others as they want to be done to*.

Here's an example: If you plan to give a present to your partner, you could practice the Golden Rule and provide something that you would like to receive, which could be a nice gesture and make you happy. But wouldn't it be better to practice the Platinum Rule and give a present that the receiver would want to receive, that would make them truly happy? Relationships work best when we are responsive to each other's emotional needs and when we give to each other in ways that the other wants. That's the Platinum Rule in action.

Staying Conscious

*We live a long time with the choices that we make.
Our decisions have long-term consequences.*

All relationships have challenges. That's okay. The key to Radical Living is to identify those challenges and then choose which ones you want to take on, and when. It's also important for us to identify and discuss any areas where we are not in alignment with our partner. This prevents surprises from coming up after you have made a commitment. We live a long time with the choices that we make. Our decisions have long-term consequences. We must stay conscious throughout the whole process so that we can make wise decisions that will have the greatest potential for long-term success and happiness, and to fully enjoy the benefits of *Radical Living*.

Staying conscious is the best way we can prevent being a statistic. That's the way we prevent having to go through the pain of divorce. After all, the pain of a breakup is difficult enough. It's even more difficult when there's a marriage at stake, especially if there are children in the picture. To avoid that kind of pain from creeping up in the future, you must understand the significance of your choices in the present. It's the secret to balancing your head and your heart, and to do so it's helpful to understand the three levels of consciousness.

3 Levels of Consciousness

Level One: Conscious

Let's say you arrive at the mall, park your car, and go inside. If you are *conscious* when you park your car, you will take note of where you have parked it. You might even write it down or at least make a mental note: "Okay, I've parked in section L6."

Then, as you enter the mall, you will make note of where you go in so you can come back out in the same place and easily find your car. That is being conscious. You are aware. You are paying attention. You know that you risk not being able to find your car unless you make a note of where you parked.

Level Two: Semi-conscious

Semi-conscious is when you *think* you know, but you are not really paying full attention. You arrive at the mall in a hurry, park your car, and go inside thinking, *I'll remember where my car is. I always remember.* You don't go through the necessary steps to remember where your car is, and when you come back out, you can't find it. You were *sure* you knew where it was, but alas, you can't find your car. That's "semi-conscious."

When you are semi-conscious
you create and believe your own stories.

When you are semi-conscious you create and believe your own stories. And as we have pointed out earlier in this book, stories are different from fact. If you are entering the mall and create the idea in your head that you will remember where your car is, then you will believe you are going to remember where your car is.

That's a story you are telling yourself. It might be a fact that your car is in section L6, and if you can remember that, then you will find your car. Semi-conscious is focusing on the stories and believing the stories to be true.

Level Three: Unconscious

Unconscious is being awake but not paying attention at all. This is when accidents happen. This is when we lose our keys. This is when we park the car while we are talking on the cellphone and we go into the mall and, *Oops, where did I park the car? I have no idea.* This is also when relationships fail due to a lack of intention that ultimately results in us missing out on *Radical Living.*

—

To balance our heart with our head we must stay as conscious as we can. It's impossible to be conscious all the time, but we can try. We can try to be more aware of what's around us and ahead of us, and what the long-term consequences of our choices are. What we do now affects us years down the road. If we are conscious, we will think ahead and be aware of these consequences. We will make choices in the present with those consequences in mind.

When we make choices in our relationship, for example, it's good to look ten, twenty, thirty years ahead. *Yes, this decision appears to be fun for us and works now. Will it work when our kids go to college? Will it work when we retire? Will it work when we grow old?* We need to look ahead and our vision must not only have requirements, needs, and wants for now, but for the rest of our life. Our choices must be in alignment with our vision and long-term goals.

Compatibility

When it comes to relationships, a distinction can be made between long-term compatibility and short-term compatibility.

Unfortunately, most people look at short-term compatibility. Your vision, though, is about your life and relationship for the long-term, not just right now. As a result, many divorces happen because people grow apart. People grow apart because they can no longer coexist in the same vision. They consider it an unsolvable problem, one they can't fix. If they could fix it, they wouldn't be getting divorced.

In fact, with respect to relationships, we cannot think of a more powerful illustration of the existence of vision and requirements, needs and wants, than the divorce rate. It's proof that vision is pervasive and powerful, even more powerful, sadly, than our marriage and commitment. When people get married they take vows for life. They agree to be together forever. They get divorced anyway. Vision is a core part of who we are. We can't change it.

If you are ever to be truly fulfilled in life, you must consider your long-term choices, which means having the tools and information to answer several key questions for yourself: What do you want for your preferred lifestyle as you get old? What do you need to achieve that? Are you willing to do what it takes in your relationship together to do that?

It might seem awkward, but if you want to be conscious, if you truly want to go beyond happily ever after and experience Radical Living, then you and your partner must ask yourselves these key questions. Coming up with the answers will get you clear about your vision so that you can make the corresponding long-term choices.

Simply by exploring it you get clearer about it.

As we mentioned in chapter one with dreams, a vision is much like an iceberg. Typically we are only aware of the tip, although we have the ability and responsibility to understand more about what's underneath. If you are not of retirement age yet, you might ask yourself, *Hmm, what do I want my life to be like when I retire?* This will conjure up images. *Well, yeah, I would like that. I wouldn't like that.* Simply by exploring it you get clearer about it.

If you are going to be conscious and get what you want in your life, you must be the chooser. You can't expect somebody else to make the choices for you. It would be nice if your life just happened to turn out better than you had hoped. But it doesn't work that way. You have to make choices. Only you know who you are and what you want. Only you can go after what you want in your life. You have to show up for it. What's more, you must look at the deal-breakers, i.e., the requirements. The needs and wants are important, but your requirements are the true building blocks of your vision.

Making the Cake

As a way of conceptualizing purpose, vision, requirements, needs, and wants, we have created a paradigm using a cake metaphor, and it goes like this:

If you plan to bake a cake, your *purpose* is your reason for making the cake. In this case let's say it's for a child's birthday. This can be likened to your purpose for being in a relationship. Your *vision* is what you want your cake (life) to look like. "Oh, I'm going to make a Pocahontas cake."

Your *requirements* are the basic building blocks, the ingredients of the cake. There are certain things that you've just got to have— flour, sugar, eggs—and if one is missing, you will not have a cake, you will have something else. The same goes for your life. If you have a vision to fulfill your purpose, there are certain requirements to make that come true. Anything else and you will not have the life you envisioned but something else.

---

*Vision can be a motivator and an essential ingredient,
but it can also be scary.*

Still, many people become uneasy about creating a vision. In fact, it can be terrifying to create a vision for some people because they feel that if they create a vision for what they want, and don't get it, by definition, they have failed. So, vision can be a motivator and an essential ingredient, but it can also be scary.

Your *needs* are equivalent to the components and processes needed to make the cake. These are things that help you function and get where you want to go and they come in many forms. For making a cake, you need a pan. You need an oven. You need to bake it at the right temperature. You need to bake it for a certain amount of time. There are a lot of things that need to happen in order for the cake to happen.

Needs are different from *requirements*. Requirements are basic, bottom-line, non-negotiable, and pretty much black and white. The sugar is either there or not there. It's a requirement. Needs, however, are altogether different. You can bake the cake for 20 minutes at 375 degrees or you can bake it for 30 minutes at 350 degrees. There's leeway. There are many ways to meet a need.

Wants are the icing on the cake. Without icing, it would still be a cake, it might even taste okay, but icing sure does make a cake taste *good*. It's pleasurable and helps us enjoy a cake so much more. Life is without a doubt more enjoyable if our wants are met. Granted, we could be perfectly happy without the icing and without our *wants* being met. However, if our *needs* aren't met, we'll have an issue. If a *requirement* isn't met, we won't even have a cake. In matters of the heart, we won't have a relationship. That's the bottom line. So be conscious of your vision, purpose, requirements, needs, and wants. And be the chooser.

Choosing Your Challenges

Being the chooser in a relationship comes with a lot of responsibility. One of its most important aspects is choosing your challenges. In *Radical Living*, we must choose the things that work for us. We want *Radical Commitment, Radical Communication, Radical Intimacy, Radical Romance, and Radical Sex*. We want a partner that's attractive to us. We want to be fulfilled. We want to go beyond happily ever after. We want a *Radical Marriage*.

We have our purpose, vision, requirements, needs, and wants, but since there's no such thing as perfection, and all relationships have challenges, we must be conscious and choose our challenges, particularly the solvable ones that we're willing to live with. To do that, we must be honest with ourselves about whether we are willing to do what it takes to work through a challenge, and whether we have the skills to pull it off.

If you are married to somebody who is always late, and you hate being late, you will have a hard time with it, push to be on time, and have conflict in the relationship. If you can learn to let go, roll with it, and accept being late as part of the package deal that comes with your partner, whom you love unconditionally, then your life will be a lot easier. Your relationship will be a lot better. You will have learned a great life lesson.

Relationships and partners are our teachers.

Relationships and partners are our teachers. There are things that you might consider urgent and important, but if you learn to let go you will see that they aren't necessarily that big a deal. Life doesn't fall apart. Life is just fine without them. Life still works without having to be punctual all the time. When you learn to accept things that challenge you they eventually won't create so much stress. You can learn and grow and mature as things change.

The way you feel now is not necessarily
going to be the way you feel forever.

In relationships and in life we must see the big picture, because the way you feel now is not necessarily going to be the way you feel forever. The conflict you have now is an opportunity for you to learn and grow. Even though you don't want to be experiencing it, you just want it to go away, and you may want your partner to change so your relationship will work better for you, you can learn to live with it as it is until things change naturally, as they inevitably will.

Relationships WILL have challenges and we must learn to accept them. However, we don't need to accept challenges that violate our values or that don't meet our requirements. And we can only make these judgment calls if we're conscious. We can only make

221

them if we are clear about who we are and what we want. We must define our purpose, vision, requirements, needs, and wants. We must be the chooser and make effective choices in our relationships.

Now that you have a better understanding of vision and its significance, let's break down the ways of achieving it into four simple steps.

Four Steps to Achieving Your Vision

Step 1— Identify your individual vision

The first step in achieving your vision is identifying it. You must explore the purpose of your life, your values, and the lifestyle that you want to live. Again, this is long-term, including into retirement.

What kind of work or career do you want in your life? What kind of family do you want? What role do you want to play in your family? What do you want to do for fun? These are some of the areas you must address in identifying your vision.

Step 2—Create a shared vision

Once you and your partner have identified your vision as individuals, the next step is for both of you to see how your separate visions fit together and create a shared vision.

Share your individual visions. Take a good look at them. Are you in alignment? Can you support your partner's vision and still realize your own? What would your life together be like if you both achieved your individual visions together?

Being in alignment doesn't mean that your visions are exactly the same. It just means that there isn't anything in your partner's vision that you can't support. It's critical that you get on the same page about your partner's vision. In fact, 69% of the conflict in relationships is created because this isn't happening. You must understand the importance of supporting your partner's vision and identify anything that you can't support so that you can adequately address those areas.

Part of a couple's development is to have each partner develop a strong "*I*" and differentiate themselves, but also be able to develop a strong "*We.*" Step 2 is where the *we* comes in. This is when we put our two visions together. These are the areas of overlap. *Here's what we want our life and relationship together to be like. It's co-created. It's not all my way or all your way. It's our way. We're going to put it together and create something different and unique, which is a reflection of us and our shared vision.*

If by the end of the process it's something you and your partner are excited about it and want to sign up for, then you are on the path to *Radical Living*. If, on the other hand, you go through the process and find yourself resisting it, then you have some work to do.

Your energy is what you want to release to the world.
You must express it.

You must listen to your feelings because they have a lot to do with energy. Remember, vision is energy. Your energy is what you want to release to the world. You must express it. Stifling it causes depression. It causes you to die early. If you want to live long and prosper, and be happy and fulfilled, and go beyond, you need to fully express and live your vision with your partner.

Step 3—Develop a plan

The third step in achieving your vision is to develop a plan. This includes addressing challenges that we mentioned earlier, like money, family, domestic and gender issues, and different ways that you feel loved. The Relationship Journal is a great tool and process for developing your plan together.

Once you identify all of the challenges in a particular category, you must then determine whether each particular challenge is a requirement, a need, or a want. Focus on the requirements first and then develop a goal around that challenge. What would you like to have happen with that challenge? What outcome do you want?

When you have figured out the outcome that you want, you can then determine the steps you need to take to reach it. Your job is to develop an action plan and determine whose responsibility it is to implement each item.

Some challenges will be individual, while others will be shared. If you identify something as an individual challenge you must determine whose responsibility it is to address it. If it's a shared challenge, you must determine how you will address it together, which includes when you will start and how you will evaluate your progress. As you go along you may need to modify the plan in some way, depending on how it's going.

Step 4—Implement and follow up

Make plans and agreements, implement them, and follow up by checking in with each other regularly on your progress. For this purpose we highly recommend developing a written Relationship Plan.

Your Relationship Plan

In creating and applying a plan, it's helpful to create a written relationship plan in the form of a grid.

Take out a piece of paper and create eight vertical columns.

Column 1 will be the *category*, i.e., domestic, financial, family, sex. We generally prefer one piece of paper per category.

Column 2 in the grid will be the *status*, that is, *Is this related to a requirement, a need or a want?* Address the requirements first.

Column 3 will be labeled *challenge*. This is basically the problem or the issue that is being encountered in your relationship.

Column 4 will be the *goal*, which is your desired outcome. *What do I want to have happen as a result of addressing this challenge?*

Column 5 will be your *action plan*. This is what you plan to do about a challenge to achieve the goal. It's best to discuss this with your partner and work it out together.

Column 6 will be the *start date*. When will you begin? It's important to space out your start dates, because if you have a big agenda and a lot of challenges to address in your relationship, you don't necessarily want to start them all at once. Spacing them out and putting them on your calendar reminds you to get back and implement that particular action plan for that particular challenge, rather than doing them all at the same time.

Column 7 will be *responsibility*. Who will drive the plan? This could be for an individual challenge or it could be for a shared challenge. Either way, one person must take responsibility for being the driver. Sometimes, when responsibility is shared, we kick back, let our partner do the driving, be passive and wait for the other person to take the initiative. This can lead to problems.

By identifying responsibility for driving a particular challenge, you make sure that nothing falls between the cracks. And since you will have multiple challenges, you will want to spread the responsibility around so that not everything falls on one person, you are both sharing the load, and there's always one person identified as driving the solution to that particular challenge.

Column 8 is the *evaluation date*. After your plan is underway, maybe two or three weeks later, you and your partner must sit down and assess how things are going. *How are we doing? Are we making sufficient progress toward accomplishing our goals? Do we need to modify our action plan in some way to better accomplish what we're trying to accomplish?* This is especially important to keep on track toward your goals.

A Moving Target

Fulfillment is a moving target.
What makes you happy one minute will not necessarily
make you happy the next.

These authors have found the love of their life in each other and are living the life we love. We have searched, we have found, and we are fulfilled. At the same, it has occurred to us that fulfillment is a moving target. What makes you happy one minute will not necessarily make you happy the next.

When it comes to achieving a dream, we naturally assume that we will stay fulfilled. But life is ever changing and a relationship is its greatest adventure. This led us to wonder, what happens after achieving our dream and finding the love of our life and having a life we love? What we discovered is that there's actually more meaning and more fulfillment *beyond* happily ever after. There's achieving the dream, and the real juice begins beyond that. Additionally, we discovered that fulfillment is 100% between the ears.

We are our own worst enemy. It's what we believe. The *stories* we create about how the world works (or should work) get in the way. Fulfillment starts with the realization that it's all about belief in yourself and belief in your dream and that the universe is a friendly place that wants you to be happy and wants you to succeed. To the extent that we believe is the extent to which it's going to happen.

Radical Living comes from within.
It's realizing the universe is expansive and infinite and
you can live as large and be as accomplished as you want to be.

But as you can be your own worst enemy, you can also be your own best ally. Because of this, the usual linear strategies don't really apply. Radical Living comes from within. It's realizing the universe is expansive and infinite and you can live as large and be as accomplished as you want to be.

To illustrate this we propose *five strategies for radical living* that you might recognize from earlier in this book.

Five Strategies for Radical Living

Radical Living Strategy #1: Dream

Radical Living starts with giving yourself permission to dream and realizing that not only can you achieve your dream but you can go far beyond that. It's that realization of, "Oh, the possibilities!"

Radical Living Strategy #2: Stay in the question

You must be aware that you don't know what you don't know. Just because you don't see it or you don't understand it or you can't conceive it, doesn't mean it's not there. Just because you can't figure out the answer right now doesn't mean it's not there.

The how is not as important as the what.

As coaches we like to say that the *how* is not as important as the *what*. Once you decide on the *what,* the *how* will present itself. And it's true. There are many possibilities and many ways to accomplish something. You don't have to worry about the *how*. The most important thing is the *what*.

We also recommend that you ask powerful questions, and stay in inquiry. *I want the answer, I need the answer, but I don't have the answer. So I'm just going to continue asking the question.*

It's one of the hardest things to do, at least at first, but once you learn how to do it, you will be amazed how much opens up for you. You will discover alternatives and answers and support that you didn't know was possible simply because you stayed in the question.

Often people don't stay in the question because it's scary. We want to know what to expect. We want a resolution. We want closure. Not having that is terrifying, and it can be hard to get past for some people.

Radical Living Strategy #3: Get support

Don't do this alone.

If you try the handle and the door is not opening and you're stuck, what do you do? You knock, because chances are there might be somebody on the other side of the door that can open it for you.

Achieving fulfillment does not have to be hard. In fact, it can be quite achievable, even easy, with enough support.

It's the same thing in life. If you are trying everything that you know and it's still not working, chances are there is somebody out there who is happy to open the door for you, or at least show you how to open it yourself. Achieving fulfillment does not have to be hard. In fact, it can be quite achievable, even easy, with enough support.

So ask for help, dammit.

Radical Living Strategy #4: Keep moving forward

Keep moving forward, no matter what.

The beyond happily ever after part of life, the *Radical Living* part, only starts to reveal itself once you have experienced some success. You don't know what life with your partner is going to be

228

like once you've reached the top of the mountain, and what the next mountain is going to look like after that. That's what makes it an adventure. You need to develop the capacity to feel the fear and do it anyway. Keep moving forward, no matter what.

Radical Living Strategy #5: Believe

This can be a hard one for people, but you must have faith.

You must believe that you can be loved for exactly who you are. You must know that you can be fully supported to live the life that you really want. But it does require a leap of faith, to enter and embrace the unknown.

Our earlier referenced scene from *Indiana Jones and the Last Crusade* mentioned in the introduction, in which Indy summons the faith to cross the huge chasm, perfectly illustrates this principle. *Radical Living* is absolutely possible for you and your partner. You just have to have faith, and take that leap of faith.

Building a Team

As you go forward and experience *Radical Living*, your partner can be your primary support person along the way, but you need additional support to live beyond happily ever after. To accomplish great things, *radical* things, you need a team.

Imagine you want to build an entire house all by yourself. It's possible, you could do it, but it would be difficult. It would take you a long time and it might not even end up being a good house—it might even fall down during the next wind storm.

Now imagine you want to build an entire house with the help of a team. You can choose people who are powerful, competent, and supportive, who are going to help you get where you want to go. Think of what you can accomplish with the right people in place. If you assemble the right contractors, architects, and workers, you can absolutely build a house. And it will be everything you had envisioned, and beyond.

With a team, you can do anything. You can enjoy *Radical Living* and a *Radical Marriage* and accomplish great things, but it's not going to happen if you try to do it all by yourself. You need help. It can be friends, it can be your church or temple, it can be people you hire, it can be a coach, it can be a therapist, it can be all of the above, but you need a support system. More specifically, you need the *right* support system.

Fire the Doubters

Anytime you assemble or attract a group of people willing to provide assistance, there will be people that hold you back. You may really love and value your family, but they might not be effective at supporting you.

For instance, when David became a marriage and family therapist, people in his family said, "You'll never make a living at it. Become a doctor or a lawyer." David is glad he didn't listen to them, because he has been successful and can't imagine doing anything else.

When it comes to your family, or others that aren't necessarily effective at supporting you, feel free to fire them. It doesn't mean you're casting them out of your life. It means you are relegating them to the sidelines of your support system as it pertains to realizing your vision.

So, enjoy your next family reunion with all the accompanying spirited discussion around the dinner table—just don't count on their advice for getting what you want out of life merely because they have proximity to it. Instead, actively and exclusively staff your support team with people who are effective at supporting you in any given area.

And guess what? People will do the same for you. You will be consciously chosen for other people's support teams and excluded from others. So don't think you're being selfish based on whether or not you choose someone to help you. You are just trying to do what is best for you, and others will do the same. It goes both ways.

It Doesn't Matter Where You've Been, What Matters is Where You're Going and How You'll Get There

You can absolutely live beyond happily ever after, and you can have a great life and a great relationship. You don't have to settle for good. You don't have to settle for boring or comfortable. And you certainly don't have to settle for bad, frustrating, difficult, or challenging. You just have to have the right mindset and a few strategies for getting where you want to go.

One of our favorite sayings distills the definition of coaching to its essential elements: *It doesn't matter where you've been, what matters is where you're going and how you'll get there.* This is especially relevant as it relates to the differences between therapy and coaching.

The life and relationship that you want is available to you; you just have to get started in going for it.

Many therapists believe that it matters very much "where you've been" and are trained that to help their clients they must help them heal emotional wounds by exploring and understanding the past. Coaches, by contrast, assume their clients are fully capable and that success breeds success. Success is therapeutic. The life and relationship that you want is available to you; you just have to get started in going for it. All the reasons inside your head that are holding you back, most of them fears related to the past, are not true. They are false expectations appearing real (F.E.A.R.).

Yes, there will be all sorts of obstacles and challenges, but that shouldn't stop you from moving forward. So, take comfort in knowing that it's okay to ask for help in creating your future and *it doesn't matter where you've been, what matters is where you're going and how you'll get there.* Get the support you need, believe that you can get what you want, and open yourself up to the possibilities that lie beyond happily ever after in the world of *Radical Living.*

You're in this Together

In this chapter we have explored vision and achieving your dreams as critical components of Radical Living. No piece of the puzzle is more important than the fundamental understanding that you and your partner absolutely will not accomplish anything without the support of the other and without being a team. You are in this together.

Often in relationships we feel helpless because we are unable to control the other person. We don't end up taking initiative, because we figure, *well, what's the point? My partner isn't willing to do X so why should I?* No, you are in this together.

If you are not happy with the way things are,
what are you willing to do about it?

Together, you must be in action. You must make it happen together. You will be miserable together or happy and fulfilled together. You will evolve together or be stuck together. You will have a Radical Marriage together or you will have a routine, dull, boring marriage together. Either way, you are in it together. It really is your choice. So, if you are not happy with the way things are, what are you willing to do about it?

We covered this elsewhere in the book, but it's worth highlighting again here: You must take 100% responsibility for your part in the relationship. It's not 50-50. If you assume that each partner takes care of half, it is easy to sit back and say, "Well, where's your 50%?" Meanwhile, your partner is sitting back saying, "How about your 50%?"

When you are willing to take 100% responsibility,
you and your partner will be an unbeatable team.
You can't fail.

To reach the level of Radical Living, you must hold yourself accountable. It may seem obvious, but we often keep score, focus on the other person, and have the attitude of Well, I do this, what are you doing for this relationship? That is not an attitude of we are in this together. That is not taking 100% responsibility. That is not holding yourself accountable. When you are willing to take 100% responsibility, you and your partner will be an unbeatable team. You can't fail.

Naked and Afraid

One of our current favorite TV shows is called *Naked and Afraid*. While the naked part is intriguing and may certainly catch your attention, it's not what's most interesting about the show. For us, the show is essentially about teamwork.

Two people, a man and a woman, both survival experts, are randomly matched and sent into the wilderness for twenty-one days, which is a long time without food, water, and clothes. Individually they are survival experts, but the couples that are a good team are the most successful. The ones that can't seem to work together are almost painful to watch and often don't go the distance and "tap out." No matter their individual skills, getting through 21 days under extreme survival conditions requires teamwork.

This show vividly illustrates that we are in this together. In marriage, like in the wilderness, our survival is dependent upon us functioning as a good team. Unfortunately, we often don't see it that way. Our society has evolved to the point where survival is not so much a struggle anymore—we generally have food, water, and shelter readily accessible to us—so we have lost the need to be in this together and to really depend upon each other.

We are in this together, no matter what.

We need to get back to inter-dependence because having a Radical Marriage, a successful marriage, depends upon adopting an attitude of *we are in this together, no matter what.* It is a functional attitude for surviving and thriving all the way back to the caveman days, and it continues to be functional and effective in life, work, and relationships.

If countries would do this there would be no war. If we all had the attitude of *we are in this together, and our survival and our thriving on this planet depends upon our being able to be a solid team*, there would be no poverty, and we would all be much better off.

Radical Living is about taking 100% responsibility, going for it to live your best life, and embracing the reality that we are in this together. It also requires a clear vision of what you want your life together to be like. That doesn't mean you have to know all the answers and you have to predict the future. It does mean, however, that you have to define your dreams and grow and evolve those dreams.

Going all the way back to the start of this book, paraphrasing Napoleon Hill, what you can conceive and believe you can achieve. On the flip side, if you can't conceive it, how are you going to achieve it? This is especially true with *Radical Living*, as you translate that into your life—and more specifically, into your life together.

234

Summary of Four Steps to Achieving Your Vision

1. Identify your individual vision
2. Create a shared vision
3. Develop a plan
4. Implement and follow up

Summary of Five Strategies for Radical Living

1. Dream
2. Stay in the question
3. Get support
4. Keep moving forward
5. Believe

Afterword: Welcome to the Radical Marriage Movement

What Will You DO?

It's one thing to know what to do,
it's another to actually do it.

It's one thing to *know* what to do, it's another to actually *do* it.

If you and your partner want to truly experience Radical Marriage you must develop the attitudes, rituals, and habits to make it happen. You are not going to live a radical life if you don't go anywhere and don't do anything. You cannot be passive. You need to define your dreams and go after them. You must create and implement the action steps to accomplish your vision. You have to go for it. We've provided a lot of recommendations and strategies, but you have to build them into your routine. You can't just read this book and put it down. You have to put it into action.

This book will not change your life.
What you DO with this book will change your life.

This book will not change your life. What you DO with this book will change your life (and marriage)!

Creating a Radical Marriage is like planting a vegetable garden. You can read books about it, but if you don't get out there, do some work and get your hands dirty, it's not going to happen. You must plant the seeds and make sure your garden has water and sunshine and everything else needed to nurture growth. And you can't just plant things when you want to eat them, you must make the effort to create a plan and plant things ahead of time. Then, you have to pay attention, make adjustments and respond to obstacles and fine tune things as you go. To get the benefit you desire, your garden, like your marriage, must become part of your life and your lifestyle.

A Radical Marriage takes two and you have to do it with your partner. You must do it together. You must hold each other accountable. It's not easy and you must support your partner and allow yourself to be supported. It will take some work, but you can absolutely enter the next tier in the evolution of relationships. And it's soooo worth it!

Welcome to the Radical Marriage Movement

As we stated from the beginning, *Radical Marriage* is a movement. It is a new paradigm where marriage is no longer seen as a drag, but as a portal to a world of freedom for you and your partner where you can be and accomplish much more as a team than you could as individuals. Make a conscious and concerted effort to incorporate *Radical Commitment, Radical Communication, Radical Intimacy, Radical Romance, Radical Sex, and Radical Living*, and do it together, and you will be well on your way to going beyond happily ever after and into the limitless possibilities and extraordinary fulfillment that await you in a Radical Marriage.

About the Authors

David Steele, MA, LMFT, CLC, is founder of Relationship Coaching Institute, the first and largest international relationship coach training organization. David is a pioneer in the field of relationship coaching for singles and couples, author of numerous books, including the ground-breaking book for singles Conscious Dating: Finding the Love of your Life and the Life That You Love.

Darlene Steele, R.N. is Director of Training and Member Support for Relationship Coaching Institute. Darlene draws upon more than 30 years of marital experience and a practical approach to marriage and relationships to bring a unique perspective that complements David's for a powerful personal and professional team exploring and sharing insights and strategies for creating a Radical Marriage.

Together, Darlene and David are examples of ordinary, down-to-earth people living an extraordinary life through their relationship, passionate about each other and sharing the mission and message of *Radical Marriage* with other couples who want to "live beyond happily ever after."

Appendix 1: Quiz:
Do You Have a Radical Marriage?

Most couples don't want an ordinary, boring, routine relationship. They want excitement, fun, closeness, love. We need security, but we also need adventure. *Radical Marriage* is a paradigm for the next evolution of marriage and new territory for committed relationships.

Do you have a Radical Marriage? Take this quiz and see!

1. _____ Our relationship is unique and different from any couple we know.

2. _____ We are absolutely committed to each other and don't ever think or talk about not being together.

3. _____ We both take emotional risks and share all of our hopes, dreams, feelings, needs, issues, desires, and thoughts without holding anything back.

4. _____ We accept, appreciate, and love each other 100% as is.

5. _____ We consciously and continuously co-create our relationship.

6. _____ We resolve our issues and differences positively and without conflict.

7. _____ Our relationship and lifestyle is driven by a shared vision that we developed together.

8. _____ We have regular rituals and practices for maintaining our connection and enhancing our relationship.

9. _____ We have each other's back and support each other 100%, even when we disagree.

10. _____ We respond positively to each other's requests and never say "No."

11. _____ We both feel safe and loved, even when we're mad at each other.

12. ____ Our marriage seems to always be evolving, providing us on-going challenge and excitement.

13. ____ We always make decisions in connection with each other.

14. ____ We prioritize each other's needs and happiness.

15. ____ We both take responsibility for getting our needs met in the relationship.

16. ____ Our marriage is a role model and source of support for our family and community.

17. ____ If we have a problem we don't settle for "stuck" and seek creative solutions and get outside support as needed.

18. ____ Our marriage is 100% positive and "I can't", "I won't", "It's impossible", and "It's your fault" are not in our vocabulary.

19. ____ We fall back on compromise as a last resort for resolving differences and it is rarely needed.

20. ____ We successfully fulfill each other's emotional, physical, and spiritual needs.

21. ____ We both consider our marriage to be our greatest, most important asset and source of fulfillment, meaning and adventure.

22. ____ We can enthusiastically, joyfully, and authentically declare to the world *"We have a Radical Marriage!"*

Scoring: While each item is important for a highly successful relationship, this is your unique life and marriage, and if you can answer #22 positively, congratulations, you have a Radical Marriage!

Appendix 2:
Seven Benefits of Committed Relationships

Chances are that if you're reading this book you highly value your marriage and committed relationships, but wouldn't it be nice to know why? We have a powerful need and desire for coupling that drives us into and out of relationships. The desire for partnership is pervasive and universal, reaching back to the origin of our species, spanning almost every culture and civilization.

85% of us marry at least once. In a recent survey, 94% of young adults stated that finding a "soul mate" was one of their highest goals. The vast majority of us want partnership and are driven into and out of relationships seeking- what? Love? Happiness? Security? Healing? All of the above?

Abraham Maslow's Hierarchy of Needs might give us a clue to what we want in relationships. Once our physical needs are met (food, shelter, sex) we pursue our higher order needs, such as emotional needs for love and pleasure, and our spiritual needs such as meaning and purpose. As a society we have secured our physical needs, and are evolving to prioritize our emotional and spiritual needs.

In spite of the high failure rate of marriage and the availability of other options, why are we still driven to pair up in monogamous, committed relationships?

There are many benefits to a committed relationship beyond survival of the species:

1. Regular, safe, good sex: Committed, monogamous partners have more, and better sex than singles and non-committed partners.

2. Companionship: We are social beings and are comforted by closeness. Married people are healthier, happier, and live longer than singles.

3. Intimacy: Emotional closeness, love, trust, mutual support, build and improve over time in a committed relationship, and are much more difficult to achieve in quality and quantity outside of a committed relationship.

4. Family: Both children and adults thrive in an environment of stable, long-term, multi-generational relationships.

5. Economics: Committed couples are financially more successful than singles and non-committed partners.

6. Community: Extended family, neighbors, churches, and other forms of networks of supportive relationships thrive on the stability of committed relationships.

7. Mental/Emotional/Physical Heath: Married adults live longer and have fewer mental/emotional problems.

Appendix 3:
FAQs about Radical Marriage

1. How do you know if you have a Radical Marriage?

Radical Marriage is unique to each couple and composed of the six key elements described in this book- Radical Commitment, Radical Communication, Radical Intimacy, Radical Romance, Radical Sex, and Radical Living. If you're truly satisfied with each of these areas of your marriage, have rituals and practices that maintain and grow your intimacy and connection, and are so fulfilled you can barely stand it, then you definitely have a Radical Marriage! See also the Radical Marriage quiz in Appendix 1.

2. Can you have a Radical Marriage with effort from just one partner?

No, Radical Marriage is a team effort. If your partner is not willing or available to deepen your connection and grow your marriage, please seek the support of a qualified relationship coach, counselor, or therapist.

3. Can you have a Radical Marriage if you've been together for so long that you're set in your ways?

We translate being "set in your ways" as preferring comfort and established habits and routines, and is not compatible with Radical Marriage. Radical Marriage is about experiencing your marriage as a platform for shared adventure and evolution, which is not for everyone, especially if you are "set in your ways."

4. What do I do if my partner wants something that violates my values and boundaries?

In a Radical Marriage each partner is committed to the other's happiness, so neither partner would push something that the other experiences as a violation. However, if you recall and embrace the fourth promise of Radical Commitment, instead of saying "No," we invite you to creatively identify what you can say "Yes" to and find the "third option" together.

5. What do I do when my partner wants emotional or physical intimacy and I'm not in the mood?

You don't have to be in the mood to become aroused
and have a satisfying orgasm.

As above, recalling the fourth promise of Radical Commitment, rather than saying "No," what can you say "Yes" to? Instead of pushing your partner away because you're not in the mood, you might consider making a conscious choice to let them in. As mentioned in the chapter on Radical Sex, you don't have to be in the mood to become aroused and have a satisfying orgasm, so try it, you might like it!

6. What do I do if my partner does something I disagree with or don't like without discussing it with me?

Use The Communication Map to identify and communicate your issue and need to your partner, make a request, and negotiate a win/win outcome. If this is a pattern and the tools and strategies in the four Radical Communication chapters aren't working (Chapters 3-6), it's time to get outside help.

7. What do I do if my partner wants to do something that is physically and/or emotionally uncomfortable or painful for me?

As above, in a Radical Marriage each partner is committed to the other's happiness, so neither partner would push something that the other experiences as uncomfortable or painful. However, if you recall and embrace the fourth promise of Radical Commitment, instead of saying "No," we invite you to creatively identify what you can say "Yes" to and find the "third option" together.

8. Do my partner and I have to do *everything* together to have a Radical Marriage?

Well, no, you don't need to DO everything together, but one of our favorite and most challenging principles of a Radical Marriage is that "everything needs to happen in connection" (see Chapters One and Two). This means you're on the same page at all times, even if you're not present in the same place doing the same thing.

9. How can I have a Radical Marriage without being selfish if my family's needs conflict with our needs as a couple?

The fourth promise of Radical Commitment is "I promise to choose you first." This is not intended to exclude your family's needs or anyone else. Conflict is caused by lack of creativity, black/white, either/or thinking, and attachment to a particular outcome. Relationships and love is expansive and inclusive, so there is no need to choose family needs over couple needs. The challenge and adventure of Radical Marriage is to creatively find the solution together that allows you to do both without compromising any more than necessary (creativity first, and compromise as a last resort). If you attempt to use the tools in this book and conflict continues to be created by a partnership that isn't working well together, it's time to get help.

10. You say to choose your partner first. How can I put my marriage first above my religious faith and God?

We would never suggest that you put your marriage or anything else on earth above your religious faith and God; the key words being "on earth." We are addressing marriage on the earthly plane of existence and wish to strongly support you to have a Radical Marriage that is aligned with your spiritual and religious values and practices. As mentioned above, love is inclusive and in a Radical Marriage where partners are committed to each other's happiness and choosing each other first (on the earthly plane), your faith and God will absolutely be honored. If there is conflict around this it is most likely because the partnership isn't working well together and one or more of the Five Promises of Radical Commitment needs to be revisited and addressed. If you continue to be challenged by balancing your marriage and your faith, we recommend seeking support from a trusted spiritual advisor.

11. You say to choose your partner first. What do I do if my kids' needs conflict with my partner's needs?

Loving relationships are inclusive, not either/or.

Conflict is caused by lack of creativity, black/white, either/or thinking, and attachment to a particular outcome. Loving relationships are inclusive, not either/or. Your family and your kids will be much happier and better off if you're a solid team. If you have a strong couple partnership, you address your kid's needs and balance them with your own as a team (and remember; there's no "i" in team!). If you attempt to use the tools in this book and conflict continues to be created by a partnership that isn't working well together, it's time to get help. And let's be clear that getting help is a GOOD thing; it means that you believe in your marriage and are committed to making your marriage work and not settling for staying "stuck." There's always a third option, and if you can't find it yourself, get the support you need to make it happen. It's there waiting for you to find it, trust us on this.

12. Where do you get the statistics quoted in this book?

This book is intended to be a "how-to" book of ideas, paradigms and strategies for couples, not a scholarly textbook, so please don't focus on the numbers as they're just for reference. The great majority of numbers quoted in this book are well known and easy to find. Statistics change continuously and are not precise, but they do give a good idea about trends. For a great clearinghouse of research and data about marriage we highly recommend www.nationalmarriageproject.org.

13. I'm single and am inspired to have a Radical Marriage. Where do I start?

David's book *Conscious Dating: Finding the Love of Your Life and the Life That You Love* provides proven strategies and steps needed to find the love of your life for a Radical Marriage. With the publication of this book we're thinking of re-naming this ground-breaking book for singles "Radical Dating." If you liked Radical Marriage, you'll love Conscious Dating. It worked for us! For more information visit www.ConsciousDating.com

14. How do I/we become a certified Radical Marriage Coach?

If you feel called to help others have a Radical Marriage we invite you to join us at Relationship Coaching Institute, the first and largest international relationship coach training organization. *Radical Marriage®* is a registered trademark of Relationship Coaching Institute and is integrated into our Couples Coach training program. Download our free *Relationship Coach Starter Kit* at www.RelationshipCoachingInstitute.com

Appendix 4:
The Five Promises of Radical Commitment

Beloved, you are the love of my life and I'm grateful for each day with you. Our relationship is the most important part of my life and I am committed to being together forever.

Though we are surrounded by cynicism and challenges, I resolve to love you and be with you for the rest of my life. Through our relationship we will nurture each other and make the world a more loving and positive place for ourselves, for our family, and for everyone we share this planet with.

1. I Promise to Love You Every Day
I know that love is a choice and I choose to love you always. Though I can get busy and have my moods, you deserve my love and attention each and every day. I choose to love you even when I'm upset or frustrated. I know that loving you means being fully present, telling you my truth, being honest and transparent with my thoughts, feelings, wants, and needs so you know fully who I am. I strive to appreciate and treasure you each day that I'm blessed to have you in my life.

2. I Promise to Choose You First
You are the most important person in my life and I commit to not taking you or our relationship for granted, each and every day. Though work, home, finances, family, friends, hobbies, and other stresses and distractions can make this challenging, I choose you first, always.

3. I Promise to Take Responsibility
I understand that my outcomes are 100% dependent upon my own choices and actions, and that my thoughts and feelings are

my own. I know that our relationship is a mirror reflecting myself back to me, and that my desire to be happy and feel loved by you depends upon my own ability to allow myself to be happy and to receive your love.

4. I Promise to Say "Yes!"

You deserve my positive response even when I don't feel like it. Your needs and wants are a gift to my growth and well-being and the key to a great life together. I am committed to your happiness as much as my own. If I'm unable to grant 100% of your desire or request I will respond positively and work with you to find a creative way to meet your underlying need. You can feel safe with me as one who loves you and will respect and honor your needs, always.

5. I Promise to Be Your Hero

When life is challenging (and even when it's not) you deserve a champion; someone who will be there for you, love and support you unconditionally, no matter what. I commit to being your hero and helping you feel emotionally and physically safe and secure. I believe in you and I believe in us.

To you, my beloved, I freely and joyfully make these five promises and look forward to being together forever.

To download and print out a beautiful Radical Commitment certificate that includes these Five Promises visit www.radicalmarriage.com/5promises

Appendix 5:
Creating and Deepening Your Radical Marriage

In addition to the Relationship Journal process described in Chapter Five and the Radical Marriage Retreat described in Chapter Eight, here are additional suggested questions and activities helpful for creating and deepening your Radical Marriage.

1. Appreciations- what do you value/appreciate about your partner? Be sure to include who they are as well as what they do.

2. What do you believe is your higher purpose/destiny for being together?

3. Acknowledge how your partner takes care of/shows caring for you (emotionally and physically).

4. Identify the gifts of your frustrations with your partner/relationship.

5. How far have you come in life together? Identify and appreciate your progress on your path together.

6. What in your life and future together is unknown and unknowable? Acknowledge and embrace the unknown as an adventure.

7. What is holding you back from trusting your partner 100%? Acknowledge and affirm that you choose to trust your

beloved and your relationship.

8. What past events are you holding resentment about? Acknowledge and affirm that you choose to forgive your partner.

9. What unrealized dreams do you have that are not possible with your partner? Acknowledge and affirm that you are letting go of unrealized dreams as not meant to be so you can be fully present and embrace what is.

10. What daily or weekly shared ritual or routine would you like to start doing to enhance your life and journey together? Ask your partner to join you and affirm that you will take charge of implementation.

11. Give permission and assure your partner that it is safe for them to make any request or share any thought, feeling, want, need or desire, and affirm your commitment to support their happiness and fulfillment.

12. Close by expressing your love and commitment to your partner using whatever words or actions inspire you in this moment.

Appendix 6: The Radical Marriage Circle

What is a Radical Marriage Circle?

A fulfilling long-term committed relationship requires sustained effort and on-going support to survive and thrive. A Radical Marriage Circle is an on-going group of two or more couples supporting each other to have a Radical Marriage.

Why is a Radical Marriage Circle Important?

Couples can go to therapy, take workshops, and seek coaching, but then what? Most couples prefer to get support for their relationship for a period of time and then move forward in their life without professional help.

We strongly believe that no-one is successful alone and see the Radical Marriage Circle as the missing link between isolation and dependency upon professional help. Creating a Radical Marriage can be challenging and the Radical Marriage Circle provides the on-going support, inspiration, motivation and accountability needed to enhance success.

How does a Radical Marriage Circle work?

We suggest meeting monthly for two hours on a weekday evening or weekend afternoon, rotating meetings at each other's homes. The couple's home in which the meeting is held is the "host" for that meeting and provides light refreshments (if desired) and facilitates the structured format of the meeting.

Suggested Meeting Format

1. Reading: Open meeting with a reading chosen by host

2. Appreciations: Going around the circle, each person shares with their partner 3 things they appreciate about them, the receiver mirroring each one, then 3 things they appreciate about themselves, which is also mirrored.

3. Dialogue: One couple conducts a dialogue discussing an issue, need, desire or request of one of the partners, witnessed by the group and supported upon request.

4. Debrief: After the dialogue each group member shares their reactions to their partner (witnessed by the group) and how the dialogue applies to their own relationship.

5. Closing Intention: Each group member states an intention for what they will do to enhance their relationship in terms that are positive, measurable and specific.

6. Planning: At the end of the meeting, plan the next date and location.

It's Not Therapy

The Radical Marriage Circle is not for everyone. Couples in trouble who do not have the skills to contain reactivity and dialogue calmly and productively are not appropriate for a peer support group and should work with a therapist, counselor or relationship coach.

We suggest first attending a Radical Marriage workshop, class, retreat, or working with a Radical Marriage coach to learn the attitudes, skills and tools needed to dialogue and support each other effectively.

We also suggest making a connection with a local Certified Radical Marriage Coach or Mentor Couple and invite them to visit, give a presentation, lead an exercise, or join your Radical Marriage Circle for additional support as needed.

The Radical Marriage Circle is for couples who are genuinely motivated to enhance their relationship, are open and supportable to the group, and able to provide support positively and without judgment.

Joining or Forming a Radical Marriage Circle

We believe the Radical Marriage Circle to be a simple and powerful relationship support and development vehicle and we would like to see them all over the world. In our experience the best and easiest way to get started is to attend a Radical Marriage event and invite local like-minded couples to get together, initially with the support and facilitation of a certified Radical Marriage Mentor Coach or Mentor Couple. For more information visit www.RadicalMarriage.com

Appendix 7: Radical Marriage Resources

What's next?

✓ Keep in touch! Access free Radical Marriage webinars, recorded programs, live events and more when you join our free Radical Marriage Network at www.RadicalMarriage.com

✓ Keep up on the latest Radical Marriage info on our blog at www.radicalmarriage.com/blog

✓ Visit Radical Marriage on Facebook at www.facebook.com/radicalmarriage

✓ Follow us on Twitter at www.twitter.com/radmarriage

✓ Get a laminated copy of The Communication Map to practice Radical Communication at www.TheCommunicationMap.com

✓ Download your free Five Promises of Radical Commitment certificate at www.radicalmarriage.com/5promises

✓ For info about Radical Marriage coaching, classes, workshops, and retreats – contact@radicalmarriage.com

✓ We welcome speaking engagements, media interviews and other ways to spread the word about Radical Marriage, just let us know – contact@radicalmarriage.com

✓ Interested in becoming a Radical Marriage Coach? Visit www.RelationshipCoachingInstitute.com

✓ Want Radical Marriage coaching for your marriage? For info - www.radicalmarriage.com

✓ Comments? We'd love to hear from you – feedback@radicalmarriage.com

Printed in Great Britain
by Amazon.co.uk, Ltd.,
Marston Gate.